Hors d'Oeuvres

Hors d'Oeuvres

GILLIAN DUFFY

PHOTOGRAPHS BY MELANIE ACEVEDO

WILLIAM MORROW AND COMPANY, INC. · NEW YORK

Food styling by Rori Spinelli
Prop styling by Robyn Glaser
Plates, linens, glass, and flatware courtesy Calvin Klein,
Swid Powell, Ad Hoc Softwares,
Global Table—New York City

It is the policy of William Morrow and Company, and its imprints and affiliates, recognizing the importance of preserving what has been written, to print the books we publish on acid-free paper, and we exert our best efforts to that end.

Library of Congress Cataloging-in-Publication Data

Duffy, Gillian.
    Hors d'oeuvres / Gillian Duffy ; photography by Melanie Acevedo.
        p.   cm.
    Includes index.
    ISBN 0-688-14721-6
    1. Appetizers.   I. Title.
TX740.D85   1998
641.8'12—dc21   98-5669
                                            CIP
Printed in the United States of America

First Edition

1   2   3   4   5   6   7   8   9   10

BOOK DESIGN BY JO ANNE METSCH

www.williammorrow.com

For David, who showed me the way

ACKNOWLEDGMENTS

Many people helped to make this book possible.

A big thank you to the chefs and caterers who shared their recipes with me—Serena Bass, Mario Batali, Anstice Carroll, Grace Clearsen, Dale Degroff, Bobby Flay, Joseph Fortunato, Josefina Howard, Michael Kashtan, Matthew Kenney, Larry Kolar, Gray Kunz, Huy Le, Karen Lee, Michael Lomonaco, Pamela Morgan, Wayne Nish, James O'Shea, Rafael Palomino, Debra Ponzek, Bob Spiegel, Mark Strausman, John Villa, David Waltuck, and Susan Weaver.

A special thanks to Laurie Jones, who first opened the door to the culinary world, and my colleagues at *New York* magazine.

Thank you to Melanie Acevedo for her sensitive and beautiful photography, Rori Spinelli for cooking and styling with such precision and flair, and Robyn Glazer, the compulsive shopper with thousands of props.

To Ann Bramson, formerly of William Morrow, who had the vision for this book.

To my editor, Justin Schwartz, for his invaluable advice and encouragement, along with Virginia McRae for her careful reading of the manuscript, Jo Anne Metsch for the elegant design, and Cara Anselmo for keeping track of everything.

CONTENTS

INTRODUCTION

Hors d'oeuvres should be tempting, pretty, and irresistible, something to titillate the palate and stimulate the appetite—anything from a few nuts and olives to a fancy salmon and caviar terrine.

This book gives you recipes that can be made in advance and that are simple (some might require a little expertise but are worth the effort). They are so good, your guests might ask you for the recipe. There's something for every occasion, whether a formal cocktail party, drinks in the garden with a mezze, or a few friends dropping in for a casual gathering.

Formal and hearty hors d'oeuvres appear in the chapter "Winter," and light and casual hors d'oeuvres in the chapter "Summer." Choose from a rich and extravagant terrine of smoked salmon layered with black caviar; delicate spirals of pickled ginger, watercress and cream cheese rolled in flatbread; sweet and spicy sesame-coated almonds; exotic Middle Eastern merguez koftas with a dipping sauce of cucumbers in garlic-flavored yogurt; mussels nestled in their dark shells with a curry mayonnaise topped with sweet red peppers; and Vietnamese shrimp rolls.

The recipes range from variations on classics to interesting new creations from around the world, many given to me by chefs and caterers over the years. Some of them have already appeared in my food section in *New York* magazine. All emphasize fresh and seasonal ingredients. My main criterion for selection for this book was that each hors d'oeuvre be easy to make at home, with a minimum of last-minute preparation. This made the choice a little difficult, since many of the recipes from caterers involved the thing home cooks dread most—last-minute assembly.

Often people spend hours planning and cooking the entree and dessert for a dinner party, and completely forget about what to serve for hors d'oeuvres, as they are considered less significant. A last-minute scramble can result in the meal starting off with store-bought pâté and cheese. This is a mistake as the first impression sets the mood of the evening.

Whatever time of the year, an hors d'oeuvre party can be for as few as six people or a large crowd. It is the perfect way to repay hospitality. Many of us are overwhelmed by the idea of preparation. The secret is to find recipes that can be made in advance, possibly frozen, assembled the day of the party, and attractively set out on platters before the guests arrive. Perhaps they may be combined with a few tidbits hot off the grill, or baked at the last minute. Plan to serve a well-rounded menu, varying the flavors, colors, and shapes of the food. Whatever the size of the party, it is best to have an assortment of six to eight different hors d'oeuvres; fewer than that makes the party a little dull. Once the party is in full swing, remember to keep the platters looking fresh. Replenish them as soon as they start to look tired or empty.

In England, where I grew up, hors d'oeuvres before dinner normally consisted of a few nuts and olives—nothing fancy that might kill the appetite. When I arrived in America, it came as something of a surprise that what seemed like a whole meal was served before the guests even sat down to dinner. It is best to keep pre-dinner hors d'oeuvres light, and they should complement the rest of the menu. Don't serve smoked salmon, then follow it with another type of salmon for the main course. Follow your instincts when you entertain.

The simplest food can be delicious, and there is nothing better than freshly opened oysters and clams straight from the ocean, served with a little squeeze of lemon. On the other hand, pulling out all the stops will give you the ultimate hors d'oeuvre: the luxurious simplicity of a bowl of beluga malossol caviar, accompanied by toast points, blini, or boiled baby red potatoes and a little crème fraîche. Most people's budgets do not allow this type of splendid excess, so this book is full of easy and delicious hors d'oeuvres that are wrapped, rolled, stuffed, skewered, and dipped.

Dips have the decided advantage of being fast to prepare. They can be kept in the refrigerator for a day to allow the flavors to marry and intensify, and will emerge ready to pop into your favorite small serving bowl. A quick garnish of fresh herbs, a squeeze of lemon juice, or a drizzle of extra virgin olive oil, and you are ready. The accompaniment may be conventional tortilla chips, or interesting variations such as bell pepper strips, sliced jícama, endive spears, zucchini strips, sliced apples and pears, wonton crisps, crostini, or pita crisps.

There is a shift from formal to a more relaxed style of home entertaining, as we no longer have the time to spend days planning, shopping, and cooking. Today, guests enjoy simpler, less rich, but more seasoned food, made with fresh ingredients, and herbs and spices purchased from local markets.

The final chapter of this book covers the return of the cocktail. Instead of serving that dull glass of wine, try surprising your guests with something a little different—martinis, punches, and even refreshing, nonalcoholic fruit lemonades. After all, you can't make a party with hors d'oeuvres alone!

Presentation Tips

Presentation is everything. It should reflect the time of year and the mood of the party, whether summer or winter, formal or informal. This is where you can be creative—it is not only what you serve but how you serve it that makes a difference.

For a formal party, where a staff passes the hors d'oeuvres, cover the trays or platters with whole spices predominant in the hors d'oeuvre being served. For example, use whole cumin seeds as a bed for the Cumin-Coconut Skewered Chicken, or black peppercorns for the Goat Cheese Wontons. If the cost is prohibitive, use dried lentils, beans, peas, soba noodles, or rice instead, preferably contrasting in color. The advantage is that when the trays are being replenished they do not have to be cleaned—just level the bed and you can start again. But this type of surface will not work for everything—sticky hors d'oeuvres might attach themselves to the spices!

Sprigs of fresh herbs such as rosemary, sage, and thyme, or shafts of wheat, will make a rustic base on a wooden platter or basket. Or, for more elegance, set a small bunch of fresh herbs tied together with raffia in the corner of a tray.

Add a little pattern and color to whatever serving platter you're using by lightly greasing the rim, then dusting it with colorful spices such as five-spice powder, turmeric, or paprika.

Raid your garden or the flower market for exotic leaves or large flowers that can be artistically arranged as a bed or garnish on the platter. Keep away from brightly colored flowers that might detract from the food, unless that is all you can find.

Use cookie cutters—rounds, stars, or hearts—to cut bread, vegetables, or tortillas. Whatever their shape, they will make otherwise mundane items more attractive.

Watch for old marble or wooden surfaces, plates, bowls, straw baskets, and kitchen equipment at flea markets or antique stores to use for unusual presentations, especially for a summer garden party, when a more rustic look is desirable.

Keep plenty of napkins around, at least three per person! Guests have a tendency to discard them rapidly.

Items in the Well-Stocked Pantry for Instant Hors d'Oeuvres

If friends drop in unexpectedly, you can always find something for them to drink, but it is not always as easy to find something for them to eat. Commercial nuts and olives are obvious, but here are a few more suggestions:

Good-quality salami sliced paper thin, served with a freshly sliced baguette

Sun-dried tomatoes sliced into strips, served on rounds of toasted bread or garlic-rubbed toast; puree sun-dried tomatoes with cream cheese or goat cheese to make a spread

Hard cheeses such as imported Parmesan or Cheddar, with crackers, or grated on bread and baked or broiled

Eggs (particularly quail eggs) hard boiled and served with fresh basil and coarse sea salt, or chopped and mixed with a little mayonnaise and capers, then spread on toasted bread

The old favorite—deviled eggs

Canned seafood such as tuna, salmon, or anchovies, pureed with a little butter or cream cheese, and with a few fresh herbs added, for a perfect spread served on crackers

Preserved Italian artichokes in olive oil, sprinkled with fresh herbs, and served with toothpicks

Pita bread or tortillas, brushed with olive oil, sprinkled with za'atar spices, grated Parmesan, minced garlic, or fresh herbs, and baked until crisp

Radishes served with soft unsalted butter and coarse sea salt

Any variety of canned beans mixed with a little garlic, olive oil, and fresh herbs, served on toasted rounds of bread

Fresh vegetables served with extra virgin olive oil for dipping, along with coarse sea salt and cracked black peppercorns

PARTY MENUS

A MARTINI PARTY

Spiced Almonds
Seared Shrimp Marinated in Lemon and Ginger
Tandoori Chicken
Terrine of Caviar and Smoked Salmon
Thai Duck Rolls
Ginger Tuna on Rice Crackers with Wasabi Aïoli
Beet-and-Stilton Vinaigrette in Endive Leaves
Raclette Crisps with Pecans and Basil
Marinated Scallops Wrapped in Bacon

AN AL FRESCO GATHERING

Spicy Asian Chicken Wings
Anchoiade Dip with Crudités
Salmon-and-Dill Quesadilla with Salmon Caviar
Seared Shrimp Marinated in Lemon and Ginger
Provençal Olives
Curried Mussels with Sweet Red Pepper
Cheese Straws
Scotch Eggs

A WEDDING PARTY

Napoleon of Smoked Trout and Arugula Mousse
Marinated Scallops Wrapped in Bacon
Smoked Chicken and Jalapeño Jack Quesadillas with Chipotle Sauce
Ginger Roulade
Mini Beef Fillets with Horseradish Cream
Thai Duck Rolls
Curried Salmon Tartare
Raclette Crisps with Pecans and Basil

A MAKE-AHEAD PARTY

Chicken Satay
Ginger Roulade
Gravlax
Smoked Scallops with Horseradish Cream
Stuffed Baby Tomatoes
Guacamole with Chips
Cheese Straws
Spiced Almonds
Smoked Mackerel Pâté

AN ASIAN-INSPIRED PARTY

Vietnamese Shrimp Rolls with Citrus-Flavored Fish Sauce
Spicy Fish Cakes with Fresh Coriander Chutney
Ginger Roulade
Tandoori Chicken with Spicy Mango Chutney
Ginger Tuna on Rice Crackers with Wasabi Aïoli
Crispy Gingered Spareribs
Curried Salmon Tartar

MEZZE MIXTURE

Merguez Koftas with Tsatsiki or Lamejun Flatbread
Baba Ghanoush
Hummus
Grilled Za'atar Bread
Cumin-Coconut Skewered Chicken
Cumin-Spiced Carrots
Shrimp Frittata or Shrimp with Green-Chili Pesto
Seville Olives

A VEGGIE PARTY

Guacamole with Chips
Spicy Potato Samosa Wontons with Fresh Coriander Chutney
Chèvre Tartlets with Provençal Peppers
Ginger Roulade
Provençal Olives
Mushrooms Stuffed with Sage Pesto
White Bean Bruschetta
Beet-and-Stilton Vinaigrette in Endive Leaves

A KIDS' PARTY

Shiitake Mushroom, Arugula, and Yellow Squash Focaccia
Raclette Crisps with Pecans and Basil
Sausage Rolls
Stuffed Baby Tomatoes
Spicy Asian Chicken Wings
Guacamole with Chips
Chèvre Tartlets with Provençal Peppers

WINTER

Hors d'Oeuvres

RACLETTE CRISPS WITH PECANS AND BASIL

T HESE DELICATE, CRISP disks of cheese dotted with chopped pecans and fragrant basil are diffi-cult to resist and surprisingly simple to prepare, as Bob Spiegel from Creative Edge Parties was happy to demonstrate to me. Plan to make them several hours ahead.

½ pound raclette cheese

¼ cup chopped pecans

8 leaves fresh basil, roughly
    chopped

Preheat the oven to 350°F.

Slice the cheese into pieces 1½ inches round and ¼ inch thick. Place the pieces 2 inches apart on a nonstick cookie sheet, or a cookie sheet lined with parchment paper (you must allow the cheese to spread as it melts). Sprinkle each piece of cheese with some of the pecans and basil. Bake for 10 to 15 minutes or until the oil bubbles from the cheese; if you let the cheese become brown, it will be bitter. Cool the crisps on the cookie sheet and remove with a metal spatula. Serve at room tem-perature.

SMOKED CHICKEN AND JALAPEÑO JACK QUESADILLAS WITH CHIPOTLE SAUCE

MAKES 20 QUESADILLAS

PAMELA MORGAN, the owner of Flavors, thinks miniature quesadillas are more elegant for entertaining than whole tortillas sliced into quarters. The chipotle sauce adds depth to the smoky flavor of the chicken and melted jalapeño Jack cheese. A chef's trick is to fill a squeeze bottle (available from beauty or kitchen supply stores) with the sauce and decorate the quesadillas with one squirt—saves time and gives you more control over where the sauce goes!

Ten 6-inch flour tortillas

4 ounces smoked chicken breast, shredded

4 ounces jalapeño Jack cheese, shredded

2 plum tomatoes, seeded and diced

¼ teaspoon minced garlic

¼ teaspoon salt

¼ teaspoon freshly ground black pepper

1 scallion, white part only, finely chopped

1 chipotle pepper, canned in adobo sauce

½ teaspoon adobo sauce (from the canned chipotle pepper)

½ cup mayonnaise

GARNISH
½ bunch cilantro

Stack the tortillas and, using a 1½-inch-round cookie cutter, cut them into about 40 rounds.

Preheat the oven to 400°F.

In the bowl of a food processor, pulse the smoked chicken and cheese together. Remove the mixture to a bowl. Stir in the diced tomato, garlic, salt, pepper, and scallion until combined.

Lay out half of the tortilla rounds on a greased baking sheet.

To make quesadillas, place 1 teaspoon of the chicken mixture on each round and top each with another tortilla round. Bake for about 5 minutes, or until the cheese is melted.

While the quesadillas are baking, make the Chipotle Sauce by pureeing the chipotle pepper with the adobo sauce in the bowl of a food processor. Scrape down the sides of bowl and add the mayonnaise. Process again until well combined. (This mixture can be made ahead and kept in the refrigerator.)

To serve, drizzle the chipotle sauce sparingly over the hot quesadillas. Garnish each with a small cilantro leaf and serve immediately.

THAI DUCK ROLLS

MAKES 16 ROLLS

CHEF SUSAN WEAVER from the Fifty Seven Fifty Seven Restaurant and Bar in the Four Seasons Hotel in Manhattan mixes cucumber, mint, and basil—a refreshing combination that contrasts well with the roasted duck in this version of the traditional Thai spring roll. The rolls can be formed several hours ahead. Serve them with the chili dipping sauce.

Preheat the oven to 375°F. Season the duck breast with salt and pepper, place on a 12-inch square of tinfoil, and fold the edges in tight pleats to seal. Place the square on a baking sheet and cook for about 30 minutes. Remove the duck from the foil and set aside. When it is cool, cut the duck breast into 1-inch julienne pieces.

Fill a bowl with warm water and dip one sheet of rice paper into it, holding it there until the sheet is pliable. Place it on a cutting board and at the end closest to you, layer some romaine lettuce, basil, mint, cucumber, and duck breast. Roll it up like sushi, tucking in the ends and rolling tightly. Place it seam-side down on a plate and repeat with the next 3 rolls.

To make the dipping sauce, bring the vinegar and sugar to a boil in a saucepan over medium-high heat, and cook it for 2 minutes to reduce. Remove from heat and stir in the chili paste.

Slice each duck roll into four pieces and serve with the dipping sauce.

8 ounces boneless duck breast
Salt and freshly ground black pepper
4 sheets rice paper (available at Asian markets)
1/2 cup julienned romaine lettuce
2 tablespoons julienned basil
2 tablespoons julienned mint
1/3 cup peeled, seeded and 1-inch julienned English cucumber
1/3 cup distilled white vinegar
3 tablespoons sugar
1/2 teaspoon chili paste (available at Asian markets)

CHICKEN SATAY

Consider this for your next big party—it has become a signature dish for Grace Clearsen of Lighten Up New York. There's no last-minute grilling as with traditional satays. Instead, the chicken is steeped in a fragrant peanut-ginger-coriander marinade, then broiled, tossed in the remaining marinade, and set aside until the flavors merge.

2 tablespoons vegetable oil

1 tablespoon sesame oil

¾ cup chopped onion

2½ tablespoons minced garlic

1 tablespoon grated fresh ginger

1½ tablespoons red wine vinegar

1½ tablespoons packed light brown sugar

½ cup creamy peanut butter

¾ teaspoon ground coriander

¼ cup ketchup

¼ cup soy sauce

2½ tablespoons fresh lemon juice

¾ teaspoon freshly ground black pepper

Few drops Tabasco sauce

2 pounds skinless, boneless chicken breasts

¼ cup mayonnaise

Heat the vegetable and sesame oils in a heavy-bottomed skillet over low heat. Add the onion, garlic, ginger, and cook, stirring, 3 to 4 minutes, until the onion is soft and translucent. Add the red wine vinegar and brown sugar, and cook until sugar dissolves. Remove the skillet from the heat.

Stir in the peanut butter, ground coriander, ketchup, soy sauce, lemon juice, pepper, and Tabasco sauce. Pour into the bowl of a food processor and puree until smooth. (This mixture will keep in the refrigerator, covered, for several months.)

Divide the marinade between two bowls. Cover one and put it in the refrigerator. Add the chicken breasts to the other bowl and toss well in the marinade. Set aside, covered, in the refrigerator to marinate for 4 to 24 hours.

When ready to cook, preheat the broiler.

Remove the chicken breasts from the marinade and place on a baking sheet and broil until browned and crisp, about 6 minutes. Turn the breasts over and broil until the chicken is just cooked, about 6 minutes longer. (Watch carefully as the sauce burns easily.)

Set the chicken aside to cool. When cool, cut in 1-inch cubes. Make a sauce by mixing ¾ cup of the unused satay marinade with the mayonnaise, and toss the chicken in the sauce. Arrange it on a platter or in a shallow bowl and offer toothpicks so that guests can help themselves.

PRUNES AND SMOKED MOZZARELLA WRAPPED WITH PROSCIUTTO

MAKES 40 HORS D'OEUVRES

THIS IS AN interesting variation by caterer Serena Bass of an old English favorite, "devils on horseback," which are prunes wrapped in bacon. Here the cubes of mozzarella, with their wonderful, smoky flavor, play off the sweetness of the prunes and the saltiness of the prosciutto. You can assemble these several hours ahead, but cover them with plastic wrap so the prosciutto won't dry out. Unwrap, bake, and serve them straight from the oven, just as the cheese starts to melt.

Preheat the oven to 400°F.

Cut the mozzarella into 40 pieces ½ inch thick by ¾ inch wide. Cut the prosciutto into strips 1 by 5 inches. Place a piece of mozzarella on top of each prune half, wrap it in a strip of prosciutto, and secure it with a skewer or toothpick. Arrange the pieces on a cookie sheet and bake for 3 to 5 minutes or until the cheese just begins to melt. Serve immediately.

¾ pound smoked mozzarella
4 ounces prosciutto, thinly sliced
20 large pitted prunes, halved
40 wooden skewers or toothpicks, soaked in water for 1 hour

TANDOORI CHICKEN

EVERY PARTY NEEDS at least one spicy, Indian-flavored dish, and this is one of English-born caterer Serena Bass's favorites. It also works well with lamb instead of chicken. Arrange it on a platter or on skewers, straight from the oven or at room temperature. Draining the yogurt overnight will give the marinade body and the chicken coating more crunch. Mango chutney makes a sweet dipping sauce; with a little lemon juice and a few red pepper flakes it will have a little more bite, but the further ahead it is made, the hotter it will become.

In a large bowl, mix together the Tandoori masala powder, garlic, ginger, lemon juice, and drained yogurt until it forms a paste. Stir in the chicken, making sure to coat each piece with the paste. Cover with plastic wrap and set aside to marinate for at least 3 hours or overnight in the refrigerator.

When ready to cook, preheat the oven to 425°F.

Arrange the chicken pieces, just touching, on two 18- by 12-inch baking sheets. (If put too close together the chicken tends to steam instead of becoming crisp.) Sprinkle the chicken with salt. Place the baking sheets in the oven and cook for about 10 minutes. Drain any liquid from the baking sheets, then place them under a preheated broiler for a few minutes, until the chicken pieces start to brown. Serve with Spicy Mango Chutney.

SPICY MANGO CHUTNEY

Place the mango chutney, red pepper flakes, and lemon juice in the bowl of a food processor and pulse briefly until pureed.

⅓ cup Tandoori masala powder (available from Shallah's, page 124)

3 cloves garlic, minced

2 tablespoons grated fresh ginger

2 tablespoons fresh lemon juice

3 cups plain yogurt, drained overnight in a paper towel–lined sieve (reduces to 1½ cups)

5 large skinless, boneless chicken breasts (about 5 pounds), cut into 1½-inch squares

Salt

Spicy Mango Chutney

FOR THE CHUTNEY

1 cup mango chutney (preferably Major Grey's)

¼ teaspoon red pepper flakes

1 tablespoon fresh lemon juice

GRAVLAX WITH PEPPERED TOAST

A GREAT SCANDINAVIAN FAVORITE, gravlax is a simple way of curing salmon with salt and sugar, and is much less oily than smoked salmon. Different herbs and spices can be added to the curing; the most traditional Scandinavian version is made with dill, which can be substituted for the fennel and fennel seed in this recipe. For a large party, gravlax is less expensive than smoked salmon, and a whole side looks very impressive. Only the freshest and best-quality salmon should be used; the two 1-pound fillets should be the same shape and cut from the same place on 2 whole fillets of similar size. Serve with peppered toast or pumpernickel bread and a honey-mustard sauce.

With a pair of tweezers, remove any pin bones left in the salmon fillets, and with a paper towel wipe off any scales that remain. Line a 1-inch-deep dish with plastic wrap. Place 1 fillet of salmon, skin side down, in the plastic-lined dish. Scatter the salmon with salt, sugar, pepper, fennel seeds, and fennel fronds. Place the other fillet of salmon on top, skin-side up, and wrap the salmon tightly with the plastic wrap. Place a heavy weight on top of the salmon and refrigerate it for 2 days, turning the salmon every 12 hours.

Remove the plastic wrap and the fennel and scrape off the remaining fennel seeds and pepper. Leave the salmon at room temperature to dry for about 1 hour, turning it halfway through drying. (At this point, the salmon will keep in the refrigerator, wrapped in plastic, for 3 to 4 days.)

With a sharp carving knife, cut salmon into very thin slices. Arrange the slices on peppered toast, garnish with a piece of fennel frond, and serve with your favorite honey-mustard sauce.

PEPPERED TOAST

MAKES 24 TOASTS

Preheat the oven to 325°F.

Brush both sides of the bread circles with a little canola oil, and place the circles on a baking sheet. Sprinkle them with crushed peppercorns, and brown in the oven for about 10 minutes or until crisp.

Two 1-pound salmon fillets, skin on
½ cup coarse sea salt
⅓ cup light brown sugar
3 tablespoons coarsely ground black pepper
2 tablespoons fennel seeds
2 cups loosely packed, coarsely chopped fresh fennel fronds (from about 2 bulbs) plus extra for garnishing
Peppered Toast

FOR THE PEPPERED TOAST
Twenty-four 2½-inch circles cut from slices of white bread
½ cup canola oil
3 tablespoons crushed black peppercorns

CHICKEN GUACAMOLE

THIS COOL, SMOOTH, cilantro-spiked guacamole looks smashing in its grainy corn muffin base. A cornbread loaf can be used instead of the muffins—if you can find one. Chef Susan Weaver suggests using a cookie or pastry cutter to form each hors d'oeuvre, making the production much easier and the results a lot more professional.

Preheat oven to 350°F.

Season the chicken breast with salt and pepper, place it on a 12-inch square of tinfoil, and fold the edges in tight pleats to seal. Put the square on a baking sheet and cook it in the oven for about 35 minutes. Remove the chicken from the foil and set it aside to cool. When cool, cut into ¼-inch dice.

Combine the chicken, avocado, tomato, red pepper, oregano, cumin, cilantro, lime zest, lime juice, and chili paste in a bowl. Mix together gently—you do not want to turn the mixture into a mush. Season to taste with salt and pepper.

Cut each corn muffin horizontally into four ⅓-inch-thick slices. Cut a circle out of each muffin slice with a 1½-inch-diameter cutter. Leaving the muffin in place, press the chicken guacamole into the top of the cutter, and gently lift off the cutter. Repeat.

8 ounces skinless, boneless chicken breast

Salt and freshly ground black pepper

½ cup diced ripe avocado

1 plum tomato, seeded and diced

1 tablespoon diced roasted red bell pepper

¼ teaspoon powdered dried oregano (if powdered is unavailable, grind in a mortar and pestle)

¼ teaspoon ground cumin

1 tablespoon chopped fresh cilantro

¼ teaspoon grated lime zest

1 tablespoon fresh lime juice

⅛ teaspoon chili paste (available in Asian markets)

3 regular-size corn muffins

SEVILLE OLIVES

FLAVORED OLIVES AND a glass of wine are a classic Mediterranean combination. Over the last few years, the selection of cured olives has greatly improved, but Mediterranean olives still have more flavor than their California counterparts. The recipes for Grace Clearsen's Seville marinade and Serena Bass's Provençal marinade (page 71) will give the olives a greater depth of flavor. They will keep in the refrigerator, covered, for about 4 weeks.

36 large green olives, unpitted
½ teaspoon cumin seeds
1 teaspoon dried oregano
½ teaspoon chopped dried
    rosemary (or 1 sprig fresh
    rosemary)
½ teaspoon dried thyme
2 bay leaves
½ teaspoon fennel seeds
4 cloves garlic, crushed
¼ cup balsamic vinegar
4 anchovy fillets, mashed to a paste
Extra virgin olive oil to cover
    (about 1¼ cups)

Place the olives on a flat surface, and crush them slightly—without altering their shape—with the side of a cleaver or mallet. In a preserving jar, toss the olives with the cumin seeds, oregano, rosemary, thyme, bay leaves, fennel seeds, garlic, vinegar, and anchovy paste, and cover with olive oil. Set aside for a week to marinate.

CHEESE STRAWS

THESE DELICIOUS HOMEMADE crisp and cheesy twists of puff pastry are quick and easy to make, especially if you use store-bought frozen puff pastry. They're best the day they're made, but keep for several days in a tightly sealed container. Arrange them in a rustic basket and serve with cocktails before dinner.

Mix the cheeses, salt, and cayenne pepper together in a small bowl.

Dust the work surface with flour. If the pastry dough is packed in two ½-pound sheets, roll one sheet of pastry or 8 ounces pastry to a 10- by 18-inch rectangle. Brush the entire surface of the dough with the beaten egg and sprinkle 1 cup of the cheese mixture over the top half of the dough. Fold the bottom half of the dough over the cheese, and press the edges with the rolling pin to seal, then press the dough gently in a few places to make the layers stick together. Roll the dough into a 10- by 18-inch rectangle. Sprinkle ¼ cup of the cheese mixture over the top of the dough, and with a rolling pin press the cheese into the dough.

Using a pizza wheel, trim the edges of the dough and cut it into ¾-inch-wide strips. Twist the strips loosely 4 or 5 times from the center out, and place them on a parchment-lined cookie sheet. Repeat with remaining dough. Place the cookie sheets in the refrigerator to allow the pastry dough to rest for 30 minutes.

Preheat the oven to 400°F.

Bake the cheese straws for 12 to 15 minutes until golden. Remove them from the oven and cool on a wire rack. Serve at room temperature.

1½ cups finely grated Parmesan cheese

1 cup finely grated sharp Cheddar cheese

½ teaspoon salt

¼ to ½ teaspoon cayenne pepper

Flour for dusting work surface

1 pound frozen puff pastry, defrosted (Pepperidge Farm works well)

1 egg, beaten

CHEESE FRITTERS

ANOTHER VERSION OF a fried cheese sandwich, these little Swiss-inspired fritters from chef Gray Kunz of Lespinasse are slightly sweet and fruity from the Château de Vinzel wine and kirsch (a cherry brandy). They can be assembled ahead of time but should be served while the bread is still crisp. This is a great winter treat.

¼ cup Vinzel or dry Chardonnay

1 small baguette, cut in sixteen
    ¼-inch-thick slices

12 ounces Gruyère cheese, grated

2 eggs

2 teaspoons kirsch (a brandy made
    from cherries)

2 tablespoons flour

¼ cup light cream

Pinch nutmeg

Peanut oil for frying

Sprinkle a little wine over baguette slices. Mix the remaining wine with the cheese, eggs, kirsch, flour, cream and a pinch of nutmeg in a bowl until well combined. Spread the mixture about ¾ inch thick on each baguette slice.

    In a large skillet, heat 1 inch oil and place each baguette slice, cheese side down, in the skillet. Do not crowd them. Fry them until golden, about 2 minutes, and drain them on paper towels. Repeat with the remaining baguette slices. Serve immediately.

CHICKEN LIVER PÂTÉ

ALWAYS A CROWD pleaser, and very easy to make. Preparing it at least three to four hours ahead, if not the day before, allows the herbs, spices, and peppercorns to infuse the chicken livers with their flavors. Serve it in an attractive terrine along with crostini, pumpernickel bread, melba toast, or a sliced baguette and a few cornichons.

Place the livers in a bowl and cover them with milk. Set aside for several hours. Drain and rinse.

Melt the butter in a medium-size saucepan over low heat. Add the onion and thyme and cook, stirring, until the onion is soft, 2 to 3 minutes.

Add the chicken livers and cook, stirring, for a few minutes, until the livers are still slightly pink inside. Remove them from the heat.

Pour the butter and livers into the bowl of a food processor. Add the brandy, garlic, allspice, and nutmeg and process until smooth. Add 2 teaspoons green peppercorns and process for a few seconds. Pour the puree into a terrine, and fold in the cream and remaining peppercorns. Cover it with plastic wrap and refrigerate. Bring it to room temperature before serving.

CROSTINI

Preheat the oven to 350°F.

Slice the Italian bread into ¼-inch slices. Using a 1½-inch-diameter cookie cutter, cut it into circles or slice a baguette or fiselle into ¼-inch-thick slices. Arrange the slices on a baking sheet, brush the tops with olive oil, and bake for about 10 minutes until the edges start to turn golden brown. They can be made a day ahead and stored in an airtight container.

---

1 pound chicken livers, trimmed
   of fat

1 cup milk

2 sticks unsalted butter

1 medium onion, finely diced

1 teaspoon dried thyme

2 tablespoons brandy or cognac

1 clove garlic, crushed to a paste
   with ½ teaspoon salt

Pinch allspice

Pinch nutmeg

3 teaspoons green peppercorns,
   drained (optional)

½ cup heavy cream, lightly
   whipped

Crostini

FOR THE CROSTINI

Good quality Italian bread, baguette,
   or fiselle

Extra virgin olive oil

CURRIED MUSSELS WITH SWEET RED PEPPER

MAKES 30 TO 40 HORS D'OEUVRES

CHEF MICHAEL LOMONACO has always thought that mussels make wonderful finger food, their gleaming black shells the perfect containers. When buying mussels, look for tightly closed shells and discard any that are open or damaged, as well as those that feel extra heavy (they may be full of sand). After cooking, discard any mussel that hasn't opened.

3 pounds large cultivated mussels

¼ cup dry white wine

2 large shallots, minced

1 tablespoon butter

½ teaspoon freshly ground black pepper

3 tablespoons curry powder

1 cup mayonnaise

GARNISH

1 sweet red bell pepper, finely diced

Wash the mussels in cold running water and remove their beards. Allow to soak for 10 to 15 minutes in a bowl of cold water. Discard any damaged or open mussels and place remaining mussels in a large pot. Add the white wine, shallots, butter, black pepper, and curry powder. Cover with a tight-fitting lid, and cook over medium heat. Bring the liquid to a boil, and stir well. Replace the lid and allow to cook until the mussel shells have just opened, 4 to 6 minutes. Remove the mussels and place on a platter to cool. Strain the liquid from the pot through a fine sieve into a bowl, and allow the curry broth to cool.

When they are cool, remove the mussels from their shells, and separate each pair of shells into two halves. Wash the shells in clean water and set aside. Add ¼ to ½ cup curry broth to the mayonnaise and whip them together in a bowl. Add the mussel meat to the curry mayonnaise, mix, and spoon each mussel back into a half shell, with a little extra curry mayonnaise. Refrigerate until ready to serve. Garnish each mussel with diced red pepper just before serving.

SAUSAGE ROLLS

S AUSAGE ROLLS ARE very popular in Britain. The secret is to use top-quality sausage meat; Cumberland is one of the best, available from Myers of Keswick in New York City. If this is unavailable, then add fresh herbs and black pepper for extra spice to regular sausage meat. The rolls can be assembled ahead of time (don't brush with the beaten egg until you're ready to pop them in the oven) and kept in the refrigerator until just before baking, or wrapped well and frozen for several weeks. Store-bought puff pastry can be substituted for this quick rough-puff pastry, but since this recipe is so easy, it's worth a try.

Sift the flour with ¼ teaspoon salt into the bowl of a food processor. Cut the butter in ½-inch squares and put it in the processor. Add the water and pulse quickly until roughly mixed. (The butter should still be in large lumps.) Turn onto a lightly floured board and work it into a ball. Roll it out to an oblong, fold it in thirds, as if it were an envelope, and give it a half turn to bring the open edge to the front. Repeat the rolling and turning process twice more, giving the pastry three turns in all. Wrap it in plastic and chill it for about 1 hour. Give it an extra roll and fold it again if the butter is not totally incorporated.

Preheat the oven to 425°F.

Place the sausage meat, sage, thyme, black pepper, and allspice in a bowl and knead with your hands until the herbs are mixed in well.

Cut the pastry in half and roll it into a rectangle 8 inches wide by 20 inches long and about ⅛ inch thick. Cut it in half lengthwise. Roll the sausage meat into 1-inch-diameter cylinders to cover the length of the pastry. With a pastry brush, lightly coat the surface of each strip of pastry with water. Place the sausage meat near one long edge and roll up, finishing with the cut edge underneath. Brush the roll with the beaten egg, and cut it into 1-inch pieces. With a sharp knife make 2 little slashes on the top of each sausage roll and place the rolls on a baking sheet. Repeat with the remaining pastry. Bake the rolls in the oven for about 20 minutes until golden brown. Serve hot or at room temperature with a honey mustard.

PASTRY
2 cups all-purpose flour
¼ teaspoon salt
¾ cup (1½ sticks) butter, well chilled
½ cup plus 2 tablespoons ice water

FILLING
2 pounds pork sausage meat
1 tablespoon finely chopped
    fresh sage
1½ tablespoons finely chopped fresh
    thyme or 1½ teaspoons dried
    thyme
1 teaspoon freshly ground black
    pepper
½ teaspoon allspice
1 egg, beaten

GINGER ROULADE

THESE ALMOST INSTANT, peppery ginger spirals are real winners, and caterer Anstice Carroll finds it hard to keep up with the demand. The *lavash*, a Middle Eastern bread, can be moistened with a wet paper towel to make it more pliable and easier to roll up. Make sure to buy the thinly sliced pickled ginger with a salmon-pink color. These little pink and green spirals look great on a platter and taste even better.

Place the cream cheese in the bowl of a food processor and puree for 15 to 30 seconds until soft.

Unfold and flatten the sheet of bread and spread the cream cheese in a square, leaving a 1-inch border clear at the sheet's edge. Place the watercress leaves in a single layer on top of the cream cheese. Then cover the watercress with a single layer of pickled ginger.

Trim the edges of the bread, leaving a 1-inch border around the cream cheese square. Roll the bread from the edge nearest you, taking care not to break the bread. (If it breaks, not to worry. Just keep on going; it will stick together again.) Roll up half the bread and cut off the roll from the remainder of the sheet. Now roll up the second half. Cut each of the two rolls in half.

To store, wrap the four unsliced rolls tightly in a wet paper towel wrung dry. Place the wrapped rolls in a plastic bag and refrigerate them for at least 30 minutes. They will keep up to 2 days. Cut into ½-inch slices just before serving.

One 8-ounce package of cream cheese

1 sheet of Mountain Shepherd bread, 12 to 14 inch diameter (*lavash*—available in some supermarkets and Middle Eastern markets)

1 bunch watercress, large stems removed, washed and spun very dry

One 6-ounce jar of pickled ginger, all liquid squeezed out (available from Korean and Asian stores)

SMOKED SALMON AND DILL ROULADE

SMOKED SALMON ROULADE is a richer and more extravagant alternative to the Ginger Roulade on page 35. There's probably no end to the combinations you can put together. How about mashed avocado and thinly sliced smoked turkey breast, or ham and arugula with cream cheese for starters?

One 8-ounce package of cream cheese

1 sheet of Mountain Shepherd bread, 12 to 14 inch diameter (*lavash*—available in some supermarkets and Middle Eastern markets)

2 tablespoons chopped capers, drained

2 tablespoons chopped fresh dill

6 ounces smoked salmon, thinly sliced

Place the cream cheese in the bowl of a food processor and puree for 15 to 30 seconds, until soft.

Flatten the sheet of bread and spread the cream cheese in a square, leaving a 1-inch border at the sheet's edge.

Sprinkle the cheese with capers and dill, and cover it with a single layer of the sliced salmon. Follow the directions for rolling and serving the bread in the recipe for Ginger Roulade.

PARMESAN AÏOLI TOAST

J AMES O'SHEA, OWNER of the West Street Grill in Litchfield, Connecticut, has discovered that garlic lovers adore this hot aïoli and cheese–topped toast. He suggests serving it straight from the broiler while still bubbling. The aïoli should be made 24 hours ahead. You may want to make it with only three cloves of garlic the first time, depending on your garlic tolerance—the garlic flavor intensifies as the aïoli sits.

Using a mortar and pestle, make a smooth paste of the garlic and salt and transfer it to a medium-size bowl. Add the egg yolk and mix well with a whisk, gradually adding the oil and thinning with the vinegar as you go along, until all the oil is incorporated into a thick mayonnaise. Do not overwork. (You can use a food processor.) Stir in the cheese, parsley, and pepper, and adjust the seasoning. Set aside for at least 24 hours in the refrigerator.

Spread a thick coating of the Parmesan aïoli on the grilled bread. Place the bread under a hot broiler for 5 to 7 minutes until the aïoli is golden brown and bubbling. Cut each slice of bread into 4 strips.

3 to 4 large cloves garlic

Pinch of sea salt

1 egg yolk

¾ cup light virgin olive oil or canola oil

2 tablespoons champagne vinegar or white wine vinegar

1½ cups of roughly grated Parmesan cheese

2 tablespoons finely chopped Italian parsley

1 tablespoon white peppercorns, very finely ground

6 slices country bread, cut into ⅓-inch-thick slices and grilled or toasted

SPICY POTATO-SAMOSA WONTONS

THESE CRISP LITTLE packets filled with potatoes and peas, and perfumed with exotic spices, make a wonderful vegetarian dish that even nonvegetarians will love. To relieve party-day pressure these samosas call for ready-made wonton wrappers and can be made ahead of time and frozen. Serve them with Fresh Cilantro Chutney (recipe follows) or Spicy Mango Chutney (page 19).

Place the unpeeled potatoes in a medium-size saucepan, cover with cold salted water, bring to a boil, and cook for 25 to 30 minutes until the potatoes are tender. Drain and set aside the potatoes until cool enough to handle. Peel the potatoes and mash coarsely with a fork.

In a small skillet, heat 1 tablespoon oil over medium heat and cook the onion, stirring, until soft and translucent, 2 or 3 minutes. Add the ginger and garlic and cook for 1 minute more.

In a bowl, mix the onion and garlic with the potatoes, peas, red pepper flakes, ground coriander, and cumin until combined. Season to taste with salt and pepper and stir in the cilantro.

Place several wonton wrappers on a board and brush the edges with water. Roll 1 teaspoon of the mixture into a ball and place it in the center of the wonton wrapper. Fold each wrapper in half diagonally, squashing the filling to fit, and pinch to seal the edges together. Repeat with the remaining wonton wrappers and filling.

Heat ½ inch oil in a large skillet over high heat. When it's hot, fry several wontons at a time, turning them over as they brown. Remove them from the skillet and place on paper towels to drain. Repeat with the remaining wontons. Serve immediately with the fresh cilantro chutney.

FRESH CILANTRO CHUTNEY

Place all of the ingredients in the bowl of a food processor with 1 tablespoon of water and puree to a smooth paste, adding more water if the chutney is too thick. You want to be able to dip the spicy potato wontons into the chutney.

3 medium potatoes
Salt and freshly ground black pepper
1 tablespoon canola oil, plus oil for
  deep frying
1 medium onion, minced
1 tablespoon minced fresh ginger
1 clove garlic, minced
¾ cup frozen peas
½ teaspoon crushed red pepper
  flakes, or to taste
1 tablespoon ground coriander
½ teaspoon ground cumin
½ cup chopped cilantro

1 packet wonton wrappers
  (available in most supermarkets)

FOR THE CILANTRO CHUTNEY
1 cup firmly packed cilantro
1 teaspoon chopped fresh ginger
1 small onion
2 fresh green chilies, seeds removed
1 clove garlic
1 teaspoon salt
2 teaspoons sugar
1 teaspoon garam masala
  (available in Indian markets)
2 tablespoons fresh lemon juice

TERRINE OF CAVIAR AND SMOKED SALMON

I F YOU'RE FEELING extravagant at holiday time, this is your dish—from David Waltuck, owner-chef of the four-star restaurant Chanterelle in Manhattan. It's easy to make and will feed a lot of people as it is very rich. Don't even think of economizing by substituting black lumpfish roe; it will run and spoil the appearance of the terrine once it is sliced.

Cut the butter into pieces and melt it in a small saucepan over low heat. Remove from the heat and set aside for a few minutes to allow the milky solids to sink to the bottom. Carefully pour off the oily part, or clarified butter, leaving the milky solids behind. Let the clarified butter cool to room temperature.

In 2 or 3 batches, put the salmon cubes, clarified butter, and cream in the bowl of a food processor, and puree until fluffy and completely smooth. Transfer the salmon puree to a large bowl and stir in the lemon juice and herbs. Taste, and add more lemon juice if necessary. Set the mousse aside.

Line a 4-cup terrine with plastic wrap, leaving overhanging edges that can be folded over the top when the terrine is full.

Cover the bottom of the terrine with a layer of the sliced salmon. Using a sandwich spreader or metal spatula, spread it with a thin layer of salmon mousse, then a thin layer of caviar. Repeat the layers, starting with the sliced salmon, until the terrine is full. The last layer should be sliced salmon. Fold the plastic wrap over the top of the terrine, and chill it for at least 24 hours.

To unmold the terrine, unfold the plastic wrap on top. Invert the terrine on a platter and, holding the sides of the plastic wrap taut, lift off the terrine (you may need to tap the terrine once or twice). Cover loosely and chill.

When ready to serve, slice the salmon terrine thinly with a chef's knife dipped in hot water, and accompany it with thin toast and lemon wedges arranged on a platter. It will keep in the refrigerator for a week.

3 sticks unsalted butter, at room temperature

1¾ pounds smoked Norwegian or Scottish salmon, not too salty (1 pound cut in ½-inch cubes, ¾ pound thinly sliced)

½ cup heavy cream

Juice of ½ lemon

¼ teaspoon finely chopped chives

¼ teaspoon finely chopped dill

¼ teaspoon finely chopped parsley

6 to 7 ounces black caviar (American sturgeon or Russian, depending on your budget)

SMOKED SCALLOPS WITH HORSERADISH CREAM

THE SMOKY SCALLOPS topped with fiery horseradish cream and sitting on cool crunchy cucumber slices make a delicious morsel! Caterer Grace Clearsen says that the quality of the smoked bay scallops should be really good, and that you should use European or English hothouse cucumbers; any other kind will have too many seeds. For a more decorative presentation, cut ¼-inch-wide lengthwise slashes into the cucumber about every ½ inch before cutting the whole cucumber into slices. For a formal party the finished scallops can be arranged on a tray and passed. Or, for a more casual gathering, arrange the scallops in a shallow bowl and surround them with the cucumber slices and guests can help themselves.

Using a melon baller, scoop out the center of each cucumber slice to form a hollow. Mix together the scallops and horseradish cream in a bowl until well coated. Spoon the scallop mixture onto the cucumber slices. Garnish each scallop with a tiny piece of lemon or parsley or both.

HORSERADISH CREAM

Stir together the crème fraîche, horseradish, mustard, lemon juice, and pepper in a bowl, cover with plastic wrap, and store in the refrigerator. It will keep for a week.

NOTE: Sour cream mixed with yogurt may be substituted for the crème fraîche.

1 European cucumber, unpeeled, cut in ½-inch-thick slices
12 to 16 ounces smoked bay scallops (about 50)
Horseradish Cream

GARNISH
Lemon, cut into small triangles
Parsley

FOR THE HORSERADISH CREAM
½ cup crème fraîche (see Note)
¼ cup prepared horseradish, drained and squeezed
1 tablespoon whole-grain mustard
1 tablespoon fresh lemon juice
¼ teaspoon freshly ground white pepper

MARINATED SCALLOPS WRAPPED IN BACON

MAKES 24 HORS D'OEUVRES

THESE SCALLOPS ARE spiked with ginger, lemongrass, and chili sauce; the bacon adds a touch of saltiness and crunch. They can be removed from the marinade and wrapped in bacon about 2 hours ahead of time and broiled as needed. Pass the wrapped scallops around to guests along with a little bowl for the used toothpicks or a halved lemon to stick them into.

3 tablespoons soy sauce

¼ teaspoon hot Asian chili sauce, or Tabasco to taste

1½ teaspoons grated fresh ginger

1 teaspoon finely chopped lemongrass

1 tablespoon vegetable oil

12 large sea scallops, halved

12 thin slices of bacon, halved crosswise

24 wooden toothpicks, soaked in water for about 2 hours

In a bowl, combine the soy sauce, chili sauce, ginger, lemongrass, and oil. Add the scallops and toss together well. Set aside to marinate for 1 hour.

Preheat the broiler.

Remove the scallops from the marinade and pat them dry. Wrap each scallop in a piece of bacon and secure it with a toothpick. Place the wrapped scallops on a broiler pan and broil until the bacon becomes crispy, 2 to 3 minutes per side, turning once. Serve immediately.

SEARED SHRIMP MARINATED IN LEMON AND GINGER

THESE FRAGRANT LEMON-ginger-cilantro-marinated shrimp are pretty close to irresistible. The recipe from caterer Bob Spiegel can easily be doubled.

In a food processor, puree the garlic, ginger, and cilantro. Add the lemon juice, soy sauce, and olive oil. In a medium-size bowl, toss the marinade with the shrimp and set aside to marinate for 30 minutes, or up to 24 hours in the refrigerator.

Heat a nonstick sauté pan over high heat. Remove the shrimp from the marinade, one at a time, and put them in the pan, taking care not to crowd them. Cook for 2 minutes on each side.

3 cloves garlic

1-inch cube of fresh ginger root, peeled

1 cup loosely packed, coarsely chopped fresh cilantro

$\frac{1}{4}$ cup fresh lemon juice

2 tablespoons sweet soy sauce (or high-quality regular soy sauce)

$\frac{1}{2}$ teaspoon olive oil

20 jumbo shrimp (about 1$\frac{1}{2}$ pounds), peeled and deveined

NAPOLEON OF SMOKED TROUT AND ARUGULA MOUSSE

THIS IS A savory twist on a traditional dessert from Bob Spiegel of Creative Edge Parties, creamy trout and arugula mousses sandwiched between flaky sheets of pastry. The mousses can be made a day in advance and the napoleon can be assembled 4 to 5 hours before serving. Make sure the napoleon has been chilled and the filling is firm before cutting it into squares, or it will squish out the moment you put pressure on the pastry. This recipe is best made on a cool, dry day.

1 large bunch arugula, stems removed

Flour for dusting the work surface

1 sheet (8 ounces) frozen puff pastry, defrosted

4 to 5 ounces skinless smoked trout fillet

1 small shallot, peeled

1 pound cream cheese

Preheat the oven to 375°F.

Bring a large pot of water to the boil. Add the arugula and blanch for 30 seconds, remove, and shock in a bowl of ice water for a few seconds to stop cooking. Squeeze out as much water as possible from the arugula and reserve on paper towels.

Sprinkle flour over the work surface and roll out the puff pastry to a rectangle about 12 by 18 inches and 1/16 inch thick. Place the pastry dough on a 12 by 18 by 1/2-inch-deep cookie sheet. Chill the dough for 15 minutes in the refrigerator. Prick the dough all over with a fork (this will stop the pastry from rising too much while it cooks), cover with parchment paper, and place another cookie sheet of the same size over the top of the pastry dough. Place in the oven and bake for 15 to 20 minutes until the pastry is golden brown on both sides. Set aside to cool.

Place the trout fillet and shallot in the bowl of a food processor and puree. Add 8 ounces of the cream cheese and continue to puree until blended well. Remove to a bowl. In the food processor, puree the arugula and remaining cream cheese until smooth. Remove to a bowl, cover the 2 bowls, and set in the refrigerator to cool.

Trim the edges of the pastry with a serrated knife, and cut the long side of pastry into 3 equal strips, 12 by 5 1/2 inches. With a metal spatula, spread the trout mousse over one strip of pastry. Cover a second strip of pastry with the arugula mousse and stack it on top of the trout mousse. Add the last pastry strip to cover the arugula mousse and press down lightly. Chill the napoleon until the mousses are firm. Cut into 1-inch squares, using a serrated knife.

GINGER TUNA ON RICE CRACKERS WITH WASABI AÏOLI

MAKES 30 CRACKERS

THIS LAYERED MORSEL created by Pamela Morgan of Flavors is bursting with flavor from the tamari-rice-cracker base topped with the ginger-soy-spiked tuna and drizzled with a fiery wasabi aïoli.

¾ pound fresh tuna steak

1-inch-long knob fresh ginger, peeled

2 cloves garlic, 1 sliced and 1 minced

1 teaspoon soy sauce

¼ cup soy or vegetable oil

1 teaspoon wasabi powder

¼ cup mayonnaise

Salt and freshly ground black pepper

1 drop green food coloring (optional)

30 tamari-flavored rice crackers

1 teaspoon black sesame seeds

1 small red bell pepper, finely diced

Using a sharp knife, slice the tuna into ½-inch strips with the grain, then cut the strips into triangular pieces and place them in a mixing bowl. Puree the ginger with the sliced garlic in the bowl of a food processor. Scrape the sides of the bowl, add the soy sauce, and slowly pour the oil in with the machine running. Drizzle this mixture over the fish and gently toss to coat. Marinate the tuna for a minimum of 4 hours or overnight in the refrigerator.

Preheat the oven to 400°F.

In a bowl, combine the wasabi with a few drops of water, then add the minced garlic and mayonnaise. Add salt and pepper to taste and the green food coloring (if desired) to intensify the color of wasabi. Place the wasabi mayonnaise in a squeeze bottle if available.

Remove the tuna from the marinade, place on a greased baking sheet, and bake it for 3 to 4 minutes, until the inside is pink. Or pan-sear in a hot skillet over medium-high heat for 2 to 3 minutes.

Place the pieces of tuna on rice crackers, and top each with a little wasabi aïoli. Sprinkle with black sesame seeds and diced red pepper.

SMOKED MACKEREL PÂTÉ

T HIS IS ANOTHER old favorite I used to make in England. The cream cheese makes a wonderful contrast to the smoky mackerel, producing a creamy pâté. What's easier than popping the whole thing in a blender, then allowing the flavors to marry for a few hours? Kippers can be substituted for the smoked mackerel.

1 cup (2 sticks) unsalted butter
1 small onion, finely diced
3 fillets smoked mackerel (about
    12 ounces)
6 ounces cream cheese
Juice of ½ lemon
Salt and freshly ground black
    pepper

GARNISH
Watercress or parsley

Melt the butter in a small saucepan over low heat. Add the onion and sweat slowly until translucent, 3 or 4 minutes. Set aside to cool.

Remove the skin and any odd bones from the mackerel and place in the bowl of a food processor with the butter, onion, cream cheese, and lemon juice and blend until smooth. Season to taste with salt and a generous amount of pepper. (The pâté might have a slightly curdled look at this stage but the texture will not be affected once it sets.)

Pour into a terrine and refrigerate for several hours or overnight. Garnish with watercress or parsley and serve with warm toast.

MUSHROOMS STUFFED WITH SAGE PESTO

I NSTEAD OF THE usual rather heavy sausage-stuffed mushrooms, this light sage-pesto version from caterer Serena Bass is bursting with flavor and is a great complement to the mushrooms. Substituting sage for basil and walnuts for the pine nuts makes a wonderful variation on an old favorite, pesto.

Stuffed mushrooms are so satisfying to eat—each is a perfect little mouthful—and this sage-pesto version is full of flavor from the fragrant herbs. The mushrooms can be stuffed beforehand and popped into the oven just before the guests arrive. They can be served hot or at room temperature.

Preheat the oven to 350°F.

Put the sage, parsley, garlic, ⅓ cup of the cheese, and salt in the bowl of a food processor, and blend until combined. Gradually add the oil. Finally, add the walnuts and pulse until the walnuts are minced.

Transfer the mixture to a bowl and stir in the bread crumbs. Season with pepper and check the salt. (The filling should be quite pungent as the mushrooms will absorb a lot of flavor.) If the mixture is dry and crumbly, add a little water.

Fill the mushrooms caps with the sage pesto and sprinkle with the remaining Parmesan. Arrange the mushroom caps on a baking sheet and place in the oven for 15 minutes. Serve warm or at room temperature.

1 cup fresh sage leaves
1 cup fresh parsley leaves
4 cloves garlic
⅓ cup plus 2 teaspoons freshly
    grated Parmesan cheese
1 teaspoon salt
½ cup olive oil
1 cup walnuts
1 cup brown bread crumbs
Freshly ground black pepper
Twenty 2½-inch mushrooms,
    cleaned and stemmed

SALMON-AND-DILL QUESADILLA
WITH SALMON CAVIAR

SALMON AND CAVIAR make this an elegant variation of the traditional quesadilla. This recipe from chef Bobby Flay is easily multiplied, can be assembled ahead of time, and should be popped into a hot oven about 15 minutes before serving.

Three 6-inch flour tortillas
1 cup grated Monterey Jack cheese
1 cup grated white Cheddar cheese
2 tablespoons chopped red onion
2 tablespoons chopped fresh dill
Salt and freshly ground black pepper

GARNISH
8 thin slices smoked salmon
Dill Sour Cream
4 teaspoons salmon caviar

FOR THE DILL SOUR CREAM
½ cup sour cream
2 tablespoons chopped fresh dill
Salt and freshly ground black pepper

Preheat the oven to 450°F.

Place 2 tortillas on an ungreased baking sheet. Sprinkle each with the Monterey Jack and Cheddar cheeses, onion, and dill, and season with salt and pepper. Stack one tortilla on top of the other, and cover with the remaining tortilla. Bake until the tortillas are slightly crisp and the cheese has melted, 8 to 12 minutes.

Cut the quesadilla in eighths. Garnish each eighth with smoked salmon, dill sour cream, and salmon caviar, and serve immediately.

DILL SOUR CREAM

In a bowl, stir together the sour cream and dill. Add salt and pepper to taste and mix again. Cover and refrigerate. Serve at room temperature.

SPICED ALMONDS

THESE SWEET-SPICY almonds coated with sesame seeds are much more interesting than commercially packaged nuts. They can be made ahead and stored in an airtight container for several weeks, so Serena Bass suggests you make several batches at a time—she can't keep enough of them in her kitchen!

2 teaspoons salt

½ teaspoon ground cumin

2 teaspoons ground ginger

1 teaspoon crushed red pepper
   flakes

¼ cup sesame seeds

¾ cup sugar

2 tablespoons vegetable oil

3 cups whole blanched almonds

Mix the salt, cumin, ginger, red pepper flakes, and sesame seeds together with ¼ cup sugar in a large bowl.

Heat the oil in a heavy-bottomed sauté pan over medium heat. Add the nuts and stir continuously until they start to smell fragrant, taking care not to burn them, about 2 minutes. Sprinkle in ½ cup sugar and shake the pan occasionally to keep the nuts from burning. Stir only when the sugar starts to melt and caramelize. Remove the sauté pan from the heat when the nuts are a dark golden brown and smoking slightly.

Add the nuts to the spice mixture and toss them quickly to coat well. Spread them out on a nonstick baking sheet. Using two forks, separate the nuts from one another while still hot. When cool enough to handle, finish separating them by hand. This must be done quickly; once the nuts become cool and the caramel sets, they are difficult to separate.

When they are cool, store in an airtight container. They will keep for 2 to 3 weeks.

SUMMER

Hors d'Oeuvres

MARINATED BOCCONCINI

R ED PEPPERS, OLIVES, basil, and garlic make these baby mozzarella balls truly irresistible. They can be made in advance and left to marinate, so they're great party fare as caterer Grace Clearsen has found. Double the recipe if you're expecting an army.

Combine the diced peppers, basil, olives, red pepper flakes, garlic, and olive oil, and pour over bocconcini in a bowl. Cover and marinate for at least 4 hours, and preferably 48, in the refrigerator. Serve with toothpicks.

½ cup finely diced roasted red peppers (homemade or store-bought)

⅓ cup chopped fresh basil

¼ cup pitted, seeded, and finely chopped calamata olives

¼ teaspoon crushed red pepper flakes

3 cloves garlic, chopped

¾ cup extra virgin olive oil

12 ounces bocconcini (baby mozzarella balls)

SHRIMP WITH GREEN CHILI PESTO

REEN CHILIES, CILANTRO, parsley, and garlic make a winning combination for caterer Grace Clearsen's fragrant pesto. All you have to do is marinate the shrimp for at least an hour before baking.

In the bowl of a food processor fitted with a steel blade, process the cheese with the garlic until blended. Add the chilies, pine nuts, parsley, cilantro, and 2 to 3 tablespoons oil and process to a smooth paste. (This pesto may be refrigerated for up to a month.)

Toss the shrimp in a bowl with the pesto, and refrigerate, covered, for at least 1 hour.

Preheat the oven to 350°F.

Place the shrimp on a sheet pan and bake, uncovered, for 15 to 20 minutes. Arrange the shrimp on a large platter and garnish. Serve warm or at room temperature.

4 ounces freshly grated Parmesan cheese (about 1¼ cups)

2 cloves garlic

6 mild green chilies (or two 4-ounce cans mild green chilies, drained), stems and seeds removed

½ cup pine nuts

½ cup parsley leaves

¼ cup fresh cilantro leaves

3 tablespoons safflower oil

1½ pounds shrimp (26 to 30 per pound), shelled and deveined

GARNISH

5 whole green chilies, parsley, or cilantro sprigs

MINI BEEF FILLETS WITH HORSERADISH CREAM

MAKES 48 BEEF CROSTINI

A WHOLE FILLET of beef is always popular at parties but can be a little unwieldy. This method of cutting the beef into four mini fillets makes it much easier to eat and more appealing to the eye. The flavors of the crisp crostini topped with beef and a little horseradish cream reminds me of roast beef and Yorkshire pudding!

Cut the beef lengthwise into 4 equal pieces to form 4 mini fillets. Brush the entire surface of each fillet with olive oil, and rub ½ tablespoon of black pepper into each mini fillet. Season to taste with salt.

Heat 1 tablespoon of olive oil in a large skillet over high heat. When the oil is hot, add 1 or 2 fillets and sear, turning frequently, until the outside is brown and the center is still rare, 3 to 4 minutes. Remove from the skillet and set aside to cool. Repeat with the remaining fillets.

Mix together the crème fraîche, horseradish, and chopped thyme in a bowl. Season to taste with salt and pepper.

When the fillets have cooled, slice each into ½-inch-thick slices, place on the crostini, and top with a little horseradish–crème fraîche. Garnish each with a small sprig of thyme.

2 pounds beef fillet, center cut, trimmed
2 tablespoons olive oil
2 tablespoons crushed black pepper
Sea salt
½ cup crème fraîche (see page 43)
2 tablespoons horseradish, drained
1 tablespoon chopped fresh thyme
48 crostini (page 29)

GARNISH
3 large sprigs fresh thyme

SMOKED TROUT–STUFFED EGGS

THIS HEALTHY VERSION of stuffed eggs is a wonderful twist on the traditional and much loved deviled eggs. The smokiness of the trout contrasts with the tartness of the preserved lemons, while the diced tomatoes and chives add a dash of color to the piquant filling. Hard-boiled egg whites make a perfect, healthy, low-fat container for any number of fillings—try the Curried Salmon Tartare (page 89).

½ cup plain yogurt

12 hard-boiled eggs, shells removed

8 ounces smoked trout

1½ tablespoons finely diced
   preserved lemon peel (see Note)

¼ cup seeded tomato cut in
   ⅛-inch dice

2 tablespoons chopped chives

Sea salt and freshly ground black
   pepper

Place the yogurt in a sieve lined with a paper towel and allow the yogurt to drain for several hours. Halve the eggs lengthwise and carefully remove and discard the egg yolk. Shave a thin piece off the bottom of each egg-white half, to ensure it will sit properly when filled.

Remove the skin from the smoked trout and flake into small pieces, removing any fine bones. Place the smoked trout in a bowl, add the preserved lemon peel, tomato, and 1½ tablespoons chives, and season to taste with salt and pepper.

Gently stir in 2 to 3 tablespoons of the drained yogurt, until the mixture is just combined; do not overwork it.

Using a teaspoon, mound the trout mixture into each egg-white cavity. Garnish with remaining chives.

NOTE: While preserved lemon peel is preferred, regular lemon peel may be substituted. Use a little less, since its taste is not as mellow.

SPICY ASIAN CHICKEN WINGS

THESE ARE GREAT for a summer garden cocktail party or a younger crowd, but make sure there are lots of napkins around for this rather sticky finger food. The sweet honey contrasts with the piquant orange-ginger-soy glaze to make these wings irresistible—you'll never want to eat the Buffalo version again!

16 chicken wings (about 2½ pounds)

¼ cup soy sauce

3 tablespoons honey

¼ cup hoisin sauce

Grated zest and juice of 1 large orange

4 cloves garlic, minced

2½ tablespoons minced ginger

1 tablespoon Dijon mustard

⅛ teaspoon cayenne pepper

Salt and freshly ground black pepper

⅛ teaspoon Chinese five-spice powder

Remove the wing tips and discard. Cut the wings in half at the joint.

Mix the remaining ingredients in a large bowl. Add the wings and toss to coat well. Cover the bowl with plastic wrap and marinate the wings for several hours or overnight in the refrigerator.

Preheat the oven to 375°F.

Remove the wings from the marinade and arrange on a flat rack in a large roasting pan. Bake for 15 minutes, then turn and brush with the remaining marinade.

Increase the temperature to 450°F and continue to bake for 10 minutes more, until brown and crisp, or broil for a minute on each side.

Serve at room temperature.

SHRIMP FRITTATA

CHEF MATTHEW KENNEY thinks that the shrimp in this garlic-infused frittata make it light and summery. It's best served at room temperature.

Preheat the oven to 400°F.

In a 10-inch nonstick, ovenproof sauté pan, heat the oil over medium-high heat. Add the scallion, garlic, shallot, chili powder, and shrimp. Cook, stirring, until shrimp are half cooked and slightly opaque, about 2 minutes.

In a medium-size bowl, lightly beat the eggs with the milk, season with salt and pepper, and pour into the sauté pan while stirring with a wooden spoon. When the frittata starts to set, place the sauté pan in the oven and continue cooking for another 10 minutes until firm.

Cut into 8 to 10 wedges and serve at room temperature.

3 tablespoons extra virgin olive oil

3 tablespoons ½-inch pieces sliced scallion, white and green parts

1 teaspoon finely minced garlic

1 teaspoon finely minced shallot

Pinch of chili powder

16 shrimp, shelled, deveined, and chopped into ½-inch chunks

5 to 6 eggs, lightly beaten

2 tablespoons milk

½ teaspoon salt

¼ teaspoon freshly ground black pepper

PROVENÇAL OLIVES

MAKES 20 SERVINGS

OLIVES, GARLIC, AND Provençal herbs are a natural combination and delicious at any time, whether with a simple glass of wine or at an elegant cocktail party. Caterer Serena Bass thinks they should be made at least 24 hours ahead to allow the flavors to marry, but they will keep for much longer.

In a bowl, stir the ingredients together. If the olives are very salty, the addition of more salt will be unnecessary. Cover and marinate for at least 24 hours and up to a week.

Strain the olives through a sieve before serving and reserve the olive oil for some other use, such as salad dressing.

3 cups unpitted mixed black and
    green oil-cured olives
¼ cup extra virgin olive oil
1½ tablespoons sherry vinegar
1 clove garlic, thinly sliced
½ teaspoon coarsely ground black
    pepper
1 tablespoon fresh chopped
    rosemary
1½ teaspoons fresh chopped thyme
Salt to taste

CRISPY GINGERED SPARERIBS

YOU MIGHT THINK spareribs are too bulky for finger food, but you can pop this miniature gingery version into your mouth without too much fuss. Ask your butcher to cut the ribs into 1-inch pieces. They can be marinated and cooked up to two days before the party, then reheated under the broiler for 10 minutes; caterer Karen Lee says they're even better this way.

Rice miso is a Japanese fermented soy bean paste available in health food stores and Asian food markets. Light rice miso can be substituted for the dark, but don't use barley miso as it has a very different flavor.

In a large bowl, mix the ribs with the sugar and soy sauce. Set aside to marinate for at least 30 minutes, stirring occasionally.

In another bowl, mix the rice miso with the sherry until it forms a smooth sauce and all lumps of miso have disappeared. Slowly add the chicken stock.

Place a wok over high heat for 3 minutes. Add the peanut oil, and swirl it around in the hot wok for a few seconds. Add half the spareribs and brown for 2 to 3 minutes, stirring occasionally. Remove the ribs with a wire strainer, allowing the oil to drip back into the wok. Repeat with the remaining ribs.

Reduce the heat to low. Pour off the excess oil in the wok, return to low heat, and add the ginger, garlic, and scallions and cook, stirring, over medium heat for 2 minutes. Return the spareribs to the wok, increase the heat to high, and toss the ribs with the ginger and garlic for a few seconds.

Add the miso-sherry sauce to the wok, cover, and simmer slowly for about 45 minutes. Check and stir every 15 minutes, until the sauce is reduced to a thick syrupy glaze. If too much liquid remains in the wok toward the end of the cooking time, remove the cover, increase the heat to high, and reduce the sauce until it reaches a syrupy glaze.

The ribs can be prepared ahead, up to two days in advance at this point.

When ready to serve, place the ribs on a grill pan and broil 3 to 4 inches from the flame for about 5 minutes, then turn and broil for an additional 5 minutes.

Remove the ribs from the broiler and serve.

2 pounds pork spareribs, cut into 1-inch pieces (ask your butcher to do this) trimmed of fat

1 teaspoon sugar

2 teaspoons low-sodium soy sauce

2½ tablespoons dark rice miso

⅓ cup medium dry sherry

¾ cup salt-free chicken stock

2 tablespoons peanut oil

2 tablespoons finely julienned fresh ginger

1 teaspoon chopped garlic

3 scallions, white and green parts, cut into 1-inch pieces

GRILLED ZA'ATAR BREAD

Z A'ATAR, A MIDDLE Eastern spice mixture, is ideal to brush on any flatbread, such as *lavash* or pita. Grill the spicy bread just before serving. It makes a great accompaniment to hummus (page 92), baba ghanoush (page 93), or other dips.

½ cup za'atar (spice mixture available in Middle Eastern markets)
½ cup extra virgin olive oil
10 pieces thin pita bread or 2 to 3 sheets *lavash* bread
Salt and freshly ground black pepper

In a bowl, mix ¼ cup za'atar with olive oil. Brush the mixture on both sides of bread. Season with salt, pepper, and the remaining za'atar.

Place the oiled pita or *lavash* bread on a hot grill and cook until well marked on both sides.

LAMEJUN FLATBREAD

D ON'T BE INTIMIDATED by the number of ingredients in chef Joseph Fortunato's Middle Eastern lamb "pizza." It's definitely worth the effort to make it. You can cook the colorful lamb topping well ahead of time, which will improve the flavor, and the flatbread can be assembled and placed in the oven just before serving.

Preheat the oven to 400°F.

Cut a small X at the bottom of each tomato, and place the tomatoes in a pot of boiling water for 30 seconds. Remove and plunge them into a bowl of ice water. Peel off the skin with a sharp knife.

Sear the lamb in a large skillet over medium-high heat for 3 to 4 minutes, stirring occasionally. Drain the fat and set the lamb aside in a bowl. Heat 2 tablespoons oil in the skillet and add the garlic, onion, peppers, carrot, celery, and tomatoes and cook, stirring, until tender, about 8 minutes. Add the lamb and tomato paste, stirring constantly until all the ingredients are fully incorporated. Add the cumin, Aleppo pepper, cayenne pepper, coriander, and cinnamon. Simmer until all the flavors are brought out, about 10 minutes. Season to taste with salt and black pepper and set aside to cool. When cool, add the fresh herbs.

In a small bowl, combine the za'atar with remaining olive oil. Mix well and brush onto one side of each pita. Spread a thin layer of the lamb mixture on the pita and bake on a cookie sheet until crust is crisp, about 10 minutes. Slice the pitas into 6 wedges and serve hot.

NOTE: If you can't find these uncommon peppers, you can substitute a mixture of 3 parts sweet Hungarian pepper and 1 part ground, mildly hot red pepper flakes.

5 plum tomatoes, peeled, seeded, and chopped
1 pound ground lamb
1/2 cup extra virgin olive oil, plus 2 tablespoons
5 cloves garlic, minced
1 cup diced red onion
1 cup diced yellow bell pepper
1 cup diced red bell pepper
1/2 cup diced carrot
1/2 cup diced celery
1/2 cup tomato paste
2 tablespoons ground cumin
1 tablespoon Aleppo pepper or Near East pepper (available in Middle Eastern markets) (see Note)
1/2 teaspoon cayenne pepper
1 tablespoon ground coriander
1 teaspoon cinnamon
Salt and freshly ground black pepper
1/4 cup chopped fresh mint
1/4 cup chopped fresh cilantro
1/4 cup chopped fresh parsley
2 tablespoons za'atar (spice mixture available in Middle Eastern markets)

Six 8-inch-diameter pitas

BEET-AND-STILTON VINAIGRETTE
IN ENDIVE LEAVES

MAKES 20 HORS D'OEUVRES

THIS IS A summertime delight from caterer Bob Spiegel. The endive spear makes a natural holder for the colorful vinaigrette. Chopped walnuts can be added to the mixture to give it a little more crunch.

1 tablespoon minced shallot

1 tablespoon sherry vinegar

1 tablespoon olive oil

¼ pound Stilton cheese, crumbled

1 large or 2 medium-size beets, boiled or roasted in aluminum foil, peeled and cut into ⅛- to ¼-inch dice

Salt and freshly ground black pepper

4 medium heads Belgian endive

GARNISH
1 tablespoon finely chopped chives

Mix the shallot with the vinegar in a small bowl, and set aside for 5 minutes to marinate. Add the oil, cheese, and diced beets to the shallots and stir together until well mixed. Season to taste with salt and pepper. This mixture can be made ahead of time.

Cut the bottom from each endive, separate the leaves, rinse, and pat dry. Trim each leaf to make it 2 inches long from the tip. Place a teaspoon of the beet-Stilton mixture onto each leaf, and garnish. The endive leaves should not be assembled until just before guests arrive, as they tend to dry and curl at the edges.

GOAT CHEESE WITH PISTACHIO AND FRESH FIGS

TAKE YOUR PICK of black or green figs, just as long as they're the best quality. Stuffing them can be a little tricky, so chef Susan Weaver suggests you make sure the cheese is soft.

6 tablespoons goat cheese

2 tablespoons chopped pistachio nuts

¼ teaspoon chopped fresh thyme leaves

½ teaspoon chopped Italian parsley

Salt and freshly ground black pepper

8 small or 4 large ripe figs

GARNISH
Thyme sprigs

Stir the goat cheese with the pistachios, thyme, and parsley in a bowl until soft. Season with salt and pepper.

With a small melon baller, hollow out the center of each fig, starting from the base. Fill the fig with the goat cheese mixture and chill until the cheese is firm. When ready to serve, cut each fig into 3 or 4 round slices and garnish each slice with a sprig of fresh thyme.

GOAT CHEESE WONTONS

THESE DELICIOUS CRISPY wontons filled with peppery goat cheese flecked with chives can be fried ahead of time and warmed up in the oven when ready to serve. Keep wonton wrappers in the freezer—they are a great standby.

Mix the goat cheese with the chives and black pepper.

Set out 5 wonton wrappers on a flat surface and brush the edges of each wonton wrapper with water. Place 1 teaspoon of the goat cheese mixture in the center of each wrapper, fold the wrapper diagonally into a triangle, and crimp the edges with a fork to seal. Repeat with the remaining wrappers. Add about 1 inch of oil to a wok or a deep skillet, heat over medium-high heat, and deep-fry a few wontons at a time until they begin to turn golden and look crisp, 3 to 5 minutes. Drain on paper towels and serve immediately.

The wontons can be cooked up to 2 hours ahead and reheated in a 350°F oven for about 10 minutes before serving.

6 ounces goat cheese

4½ tablespoons chopped chives

1 teaspoon freshly ground black pepper

20 wonton wrappers

Vegetable oil for frying

CHÈVRE TARTLETS WITH PROVENÇAL PEPPERS

THE FLAVORS OF tangy goat cheese and sweet red and green bell peppers spiked with *herbes de Provence* work together so well. Baked wonton shells make crisp and crunchy containers for these tartlets. They'll keep for at least a month in an airtight container and make great standbys for the unexpected guest.

Butter-flavored cooking spray

18 to 20 wonton wrappers,
   2½ inches square

3 tablespoons olive oil

1 cup julienned red bell pepper

1 cup julienned green bell pepper

1 cup thinly sliced onion

½ teaspoon *herbes de Provence*

Salt and freshly ground black pepper

1 large clove garlic, minced

4 ounces goat cheese

¼ cup heavy cream

¼ teaspoon ground white pepper

Preheat the oven to 350°F.

Spray a nonstick mini muffin tin with the cooking spray. Press the wrappers into each mold and spray with a light coating again. Bake for 7 to 10 minutes or until light brown. Remove the shells from the muffin tin and set aside to cool.

Heat the olive oil in a small saucepan over low heat. Add the peppers, onion, *herbes de Provence*, salt, and pepper and cook over low heat for about 40 minutes. Add the garlic and continue cooking for a few more minutes. Remove from the heat and set aside to cool. Drain the oil that separates from the peppers.

Reduce the oven temperature to 250°F.

In a small bowl, combine the goat cheese with half the cream and the white pepper. Depending on how soft the goat cheese feels, mix in the remaining cream until the mixture is smooth.

Take each wonton shell and spoon in about ½ teaspoon of the goat cheese mixture, enough to cover the base of the shell. Top with a teaspoon of the pepper mixture.

Place the tartlets on a baking sheet and bake in the oven for 10 minutes until warmed through. Serve immediately.

VIETNAMESE SHRIMP ROLLS

SHREDDED VEGETABLES, CHICKEN, and rice vermicelli wrapped in delicate, soft spring-roll skins (available in Asian markets) are fresh, crunchy, and healthful. Keep the filling as compact and tight as possible while forming the rolls. They're best served immediately but will stay fresh for a couple of hours if wrapped tightly in plastic and kept at room temperature. Huy Le, chef-owner of Indochine, suggests serving them with Citrus-Flavored Fish Sauce.

Eight 12½-inch-diameter spring-roll
   skins
8 quarter-round spring-roll skins
   (6½-inch-radius)
8 leaves iceberg lettuce, hard parts
   removed
2 cups fresh bean sprouts
½ cup mint leaves, stems removed
1 large whole chicken breast
   (about 1 pound), poached or
   panfried, sliced on the diagonal
   into ½-inch strips and cooled to
   room temperature
2 cups cooked rice vermicelli, cooled
32 medium-size shrimp, cooked,
   shelled, and deveined
8 Chinese chives (optional)
Citrus-Flavored Fish Sauce
   (recipe follows)

Lay a round spring-roll skin on a dry towel. Dip your hands in warm water and wet both sides of the skin evenly. Dip one of the quarter-round spring-roll skins into a shallow bowl of warm water and place on top of the round, 1 inch from the upper edge, pointed toward the center. Cover with another dry towel and repeat with the seven remaining skins, making a stack of alternating towels and wrappers.

Flip over the stack. Remove the top towel carefully, and place a lettuce leaf on the lower third of the wrapper. Layer first with bean sprouts, then mint leaves, then chicken strips, and finally vermicelli. Fold the left and right edges of the skin toward the center.

Place four shrimp alongside one another, evenly spaced, on the upper third of the wrapper. Gently roll the whole assembly very tightly, slipping a piece of Chinese chive inside the roll just before reaching the shrimp, with one inch of chive sticking out the end of the roll.

Cut the roll in half, then slice each half again on the diagonal. Stand each roll on end on a platter and serve with the citrus-flavored fish sauce in a small dipping bowl.

NOTE: Substitute coriander for the mint; firm, seasoned tofu for the chicken; and shredded carrots, jícama, and watercress for the rice vermicelli; or try your own combinations.

CITRUS-FLAVORED FISH SAUCE

In a small bowl, stir together the *nuoc mam,* lime juice, orange juice, sugar, garlic, and chili paste with ½ cup water. When well combined, add the shredded carrot and serve.

¼ cup *nuoc mam* (Vietnamese fish sauce; available at Asian markets)
¼ cup fresh lime juice
¼ cup orange juice
¼ cup sugar
1 clove garlic, crushed
½ teaspoon chili paste or dash of cayenne pepper
⅛ cup shredded carrot

SCOTCH EGGS

MAKES 24 HORS D'OEUVRES

THIS WELL-KNOWN BAR food can be found in many British pubs, sadly often served chilled and past its prime. However, when freshly made with a good-quality sausage meat, the eggs make delicious finger food. Try substituting quail eggs for a smaller and more elegant version.

2 tablespoons flour
6 small hard-boiled eggs, shells
   removed
Salt and freshly ground black pepper
1½ pounds good-quality
   sausage meat
1 large egg, beaten
1½ cups Japanese breadcrumbs
   (panko) or fresh breadcrumbs
Vegetable or canola oil for deep
   frying

Sprinkle the flour over a plate and roll the eggs in the flour to coat lightly.

Season the sausage meat with salt and pepper and divide into 6 equal portions. Flatten each portion with your fingers until it is about ½ inch thick. Place one hard-boiled egg on the sausage meat and, using your fingers, wrap the meat around the egg until it is completely encased and the sausage meat surface is smooth. It is much easier to shape the sausage meat with wet hands. Repeat with the remaining eggs.

Roll each sausage-coated egg in the beaten egg and then in the breadcrumbs until coated. The Scotch eggs can be chilled at this stage until ready to cook.

Heat 2 to 3 inches of oil in a medium-size saucepan and deep-fry 2 to 3 Scotch eggs at a time until golden brown and crisp, 6 to 7 minutes. If the eggs brown too quickly, reduce the heat as necessary or else the sausage meat will not be cooked through. Drain on paper towels. Repeat with the remaining Scotch eggs.

Allow to cool for about 10 minutes before cutting into quarters. Serve warm or at room temperature.

CUMIN-SPICED CARROTS

MAKES 10 SERVINGS

CARROTS MIGHT SEEM a dull, everyday vegetable, but chef Matthew Kenney's version of these Moroccan carrots spiced with cumin and mint are anything but.

Bring ¼ cup of water to a boil in a large skillet. Add the honey and 2 teaspoons salt and stir. Add the carrots and cook, stirring occasionally, until tender and the liquid has evaporated.

Stir the cumin powder, olive oil, and lemon juice with the carrots and toss together until the carrots are coated. Adjust the seasoning to taste. Arrange them on a platter and garnish with mint.

⅔ cup orange blossom honey
Salt and freshly ground black pepper
2 pounds carrots, cut on the bias
  ¼ inch thick
2¼ teaspoons cumin powder
3 tablespoons extra virgin olive oil
1½ tablespoons fresh lemon juice

GARNISH
2 tablespoons chopped mint

ANCHOIADE DIP WITH CRUDITÉS

MAKES ABOUT 2½ CUPS

F YOU LOVE anchovies, you'll adore this herb-infused Provençal dip. Chef Debra Ponzek thinks it's much lighter than creamy dips and goes well with a basket full of whatever vegetables are in peak condition—yellow tomatoes, fennel, mushrooms, radishes, cauliflower, endive, and of course Niçoise olives. For a change of pace, arrange an all-green basket, or a red, white, and green basket, or a single vegetable such as fennel.

2 ounces (2 tins) anchovy fillets,
    drained
2 cups extra virgin olive oil
3 cloves garlic
1 tablespoon fresh thyme leaves
1½ tablespoons Dijon mustard
1½ tablespoons chopped fresh basil
Salt and freshly ground black pepper

Crudités (raw vegetables)

Combine the anchovy fillets, olive oil, garlic, thyme, mustard, basil, salt, and pepper in a blender or the bowl of a food processor, and puree until smooth. Pour it into a bowl, and serve with a basket of raw vegetables and braided bread to dip into it.

CURRIED SALMON TARTARE

MAKES 48 HORS D'OEUVRES

THIS LIGHTLY CURRIED salmon tartare, mixed with diced crisp cucumber and served on crunchy mini pappadams, is a light, refreshing, and unusual combination from chef John Villa. It can be made several hours ahead and assembled just before serving, or serve it in a bowl, surrounded by the pappadams for guests to help themselves. The mini pappadams, which are paper-thin crisp breads made from urad dal, can be found in most Indian food stores. If they're unavailable, substitute slices of hothouse cucumber cut in ½-inch rounds.

Heat the oil in a small skillet over medium heat, add the onion, and cook it for 1 to 2 minutes. Add the curry powder, apple, and banana and cook for 4 to 5 minutes, stirring continuously. Add 1½ tablespoons water and cook for 4 minutes more, stirring. Remove from the heat and set aside until cool. (Make sure the curry sauce is cool before blending with the mayonnaise or the mayonnaise will separate.)

Add the curry mixture, mayonnaise, sour cream, salt, and pepper to the bowl of a food processor and blend until smooth. Add a little more water if the curry sauce is too thick. Set aside.

Cut the salmon into ¼-inch dice and place in a very cold bowl. Add the cucumber, 1 tablespoon chives, ½ cup curry sauce, lemon juice, Tabasco, and salt. Adjust seasoning with more Tabasco, lemon juice, and salt to taste. Cover and place in the refrigerator until ready to assemble. This can be done up to 3 hours in advance.

Heat ½ inch oil in a small skillet over medium heat. When hot, add 2 or 3 pappadams at a time, turning them over when they start to curl. Cook until bubbles appear, or until they start to turn golden brown, about 20 seconds. Do not allow them to get too dark or they will have a burnt flavor. Remove and drain on a paper towel. Keep them in a warm oven until ready to use, up to 2 hours; this will dry them out and keep them crisp.

Arrange 1 teaspoonful of the salmon tartare on each mini pappadam and garnish with the remaining chopped chives.

1 teaspoon vegetable oil

2 teaspoons finely diced onion

1 teaspoon Madras curry powder

2 teaspoons finely diced apple

½ banana, finely diced

1½ tablespoons mayonnaise

2 teaspoons sour cream

Salt and freshly ground black pepper

12 ounces salmon, high quality, skinned and boned

½ cup cucumber, peeled, seeded, cut in ⅛-inch dice

2 tablespoons finely chopped chives

Juice of ½ small lemon

8 shots Tabasco, or to taste

1 package plain mini pappadams, 1¼ inches in diameter

Vegetable oil for frying pappadams

SHIITAKE MUSHROOM, ARUGULA, AND YELLOW SQUASH FOCACCIA

FOCACCIA IS A great Italian peasant bread, and topped with interesting vegetables it is especially good for hungry guests. Bob Spiegel from Creative Edge Parties suggests serving it hot or at room temperature. If you don't have time to make your own pizza dough, it can be purchased at any pizzeria or supermarket. It is best if purchased on the day it is to be used.

⅓ cup extra virgin olive oil

1 pound fresh uncooked pizza dough, at room temperature

2 teaspoons kosher salt

1 bunch arugula, roughly chopped

2 yellow squash, halved and sliced thin

6 shiitake mushroom caps, sliced very thin

2 teaspoons freshly ground black pepper

Preheat oven to 450°F.

Sprinkle 1 tablespoon oil onto a cookie sheet. Either roll or press (with your hand) the pizza dough onto the cookie sheet until it is about ½ inch thick. Sprinkle with 1 teaspoon salt, then layer with the arugula, followed by the squash and the mushrooms, all the way to the edges of the dough. Drizzle with the remaining oil and sprinkle with the remaining salt and pepper.

Bake for 20 minutes, or until the underside of the focaccia is golden brown. Cut into 1½-inch squares.

HUMMUS

THE GARNISH OF the diced red onion and pine nuts from chef Joseph Fortunato makes a pleasant contrast to the smooth texture of the hummus. Canned chickpeas work just as well and they certainly save a lot of time. Tahini, an essential ingredient in Middle Eastern food, is a sesame seed paste that can be found in gourmet and health food stores as well as Middle Eastern markets.

6 cloves garlic

5 tablespoons extra virgin olive oil

24-ounce can of chickpeas, drained, liquid reserved

6 tablespoons fresh lemon juice

¼ cup tahini (sesame seed paste)

2 teaspoons ground coriander

2 teaspoons ground cumin

Salt and freshly ground black pepper

GARNISH

1 tablespoon pine nuts

1 tablespoon diced red onion

1 tablespoon chopped parsley

Preheat the oven to 350°F.

Mix the garlic with 3 tablespoons oil in a small metal bowl and roast it in the oven for about 30 minutes until soft. Put the garlic, 2 tablespoons of oil from the roasted garlic, chickpeas, 4 tablespoons lemon juice, and ¼ of the reserved liquid from the chickpeas in a food processor, and puree until smooth. Add the tahini, coriander, and cumin. Puree again until all the ingredients are fully incorporated and the mixture is smooth. Season with salt and pepper.

Place the pine nuts in a small cast-iron skillet and toast over medium heat for 2 to 3 minutes, stirring occasionally until lightly browned.

Strain the hummus through a fine sieve and into a shallow bowl. Make a small well in the center, using the back of a spoon; garnish with pine nuts, onion, parsley, and the remaining lemon juice and olive oil. Serve with the Grilled Za'atar Bread on page 74.

BABA GHANOUSH

THE WONDERFUL SMOKY flavor of eggplant grilled on the barbecue and the addition of yogurt and tahini make this delicious, creamy Middle Eastern dip worth all the effort, even though you can find it in many supermarkets today. Chef Matthew Kenney suggests making it ahead to allow the flavors to meld and improve.

Pierce each eggplant all over with a toothpick. Place the eggplants on a hot barbecue and grill until the skin is charred and collapsed (a charcoal grill will give them a smoky flavor, but the charring can be accomplished in a broiler). Remove them from the heat and set aside to cool.

When cool enough to handle, remove the skin and cut the eggplants open to remove and discard the seeds. Puree the flesh in a food processor. Crush the garlic with ½ teaspoon salt using the flat side of a heavy knife and add to the food processor along with the tahini, yogurt, lemon juice, cumin, and oil and pulse until smooth. Season to taste with salt and pepper. Pour into a bowl and garnish with parsley and tomato. Serve with the Grilled Za'atar Bread on page 74.

2 large eggplants

2 large cloves garlic

Salt

2 tablespoons tahini (sesame seed paste)

1 tablespoon plain yogurt

1 tablespoon fresh lemon juice

1 teaspoon cumin

3 tablespoons extra virgin olive oil

Freshly ground black pepper

GARNISH
Chopped parsley and diced tomato

SPICY INDIAN FISH CAKES

THESE FISH CAKES are a fragrant Indian take on crab cakes, flavored with coriander, ginger, and cumin and served with a fresh cilantro dipping chutney. Try coating the fish cakes with Japanese bread crumbs, available from Japanese food shops, for a crunchier finish.

10 ounces cod fillet

1 medium potato, boiled, skin removed

½ beaten egg

¾ teaspoon toasted cumin seeds

¾ teaspoon ground coriander

⅛ teaspoon cayenne pepper

¼ cup minced onion

1 teaspoon minced fresh ginger

¼ cup chopped cilantro

1 teaspoon finely minced green chilies, seeds removed

½ teaspoon garam masala

Salt

1½ cups Japanese breadcrumbs (panko), or regular breadcrumbs

Vegetable oil for frying

Fresh Cilantro Chutney (page 39)

Place the fish in a saucepan, cover with 1 cup water, bring to a boil, and poach for about 7 minutes, until the fish is just cooked. Remove the fish from the water and place it in a bowl. When the fish is cool, add the potato, egg, cumin seeds, ground coriander, cayenne, onion, ginger, cilantro, chilies, garam masala, and salt to taste; mash together with a fork until the mixture is smooth. Form into 1-inch-diameter balls, place on a tray, and flatten to about ⅓ inch deep (or fill a 1½-inch metal ring ½ inch deep with the mixture and slide the ring away). Dip in Japanese breadcrumbs. Chill in the refrigerator for an hour, or until ready to cook.

Heat ½ inch of oil in a skillet over medium heat. When hot, fry 6 to 8 cakes at a time until golden brown and crisp on both sides. Place them on paper towels to drain the excess oil. Serve hot with Fresh Cilantro Chutney.

WHITE BEAN BRUSCHETTA

MANY BRITS HAVE fond memories of beans on toast. You might call chef Mario Batali's creation the Italian version, with a little more sophistication! It can be put together with ingredients found in most kitchens—bread, garlic, oil, balsamic vinegar, red pepper flakes—even canned beans in an emergency. If you're pressed for time, it can be served soon after being prepared, but the flavors of rosemary and garlic really need several hours to penetrate.

Gently toss together the beans, garlic, rosemary, olive oil, vinegar, and red pepper flakes in a medium-size bowl, taking care not to break up the beans. Let the bean mixture stand, covered, for several hours at room temperature.

Slice the bread ⅓ inch thick and grill or toast. Cut each slice in half and spoon the beans onto the slices.

1 can cannellini beans, drained and rinsed
1 clove garlic, minced
2 to 3 teaspoons chopped fresh rosemary leaves
¼ cup extra virgin olive oil
1 teaspoon balsamic vinegar
½ teaspoon crushed red pepper flakes
1 loaf of country bread

STUFFED BABY TOMATOES

WAYNE NISH, CHEF and co-owner of March restaurant, likes to stuff miniature tomatoes with three different fillings—mascarpone and chopped almonds; rolls of prosciutto di Parma; and diced taleggio cheese topped with a basil leaf. These tomatoes make a pleasant change and look like jewels on a platter. They can be assembled several hours ahead of the party, but don't refrigerate them.

1 pint each red and yellow pear
    tomatoes
½ cup mascarpone
2 tablespoons slivered almonds,
    chopped
¼ pound prosciutto di Parma
¼ pound taleggio cheese
1 small bunch basil

Halve each tomato lengthwise, and scoop out pulp and seeds with a tiny melon baller or espresso spoon. Set them cut-side down on a paper towel to drain.

Mix the mascarpone with chopped almonds in a small bowl. Cut the prosciutto in strips 3 inches long and ½ inch wide, and roll it up. Cut the taleggio into ½-inch cubes.

Divide the tomato halves into 3 batches. Fill one batch with the mascarpone mixture, one with the prosciutto rolls, and the third with the taleggio cubes; top each taleggio cube with a tiny basil leaf. Arrange the tomato halves on a platter.

CUMIN-COCONUT SKEWERED CHICKEN

MAKES 30 HORS D'OEUVRES

THESE TENDER STRIPS of chicken get their delectable flavor and punch from the contrast between the spicy cumin and the sweet coconut milk. Chef Michael Kashtan of Fletcher Morgan suggests baking them in the oven instead of cooking in a skillet for a large party.

Combine the garlic, cumin, chili powder, coriander, paprika, coconut milk, brown sugar, and salt in a medium-size bowl.

Slice each chicken breast into 10 pieces by first cutting it in half horizontally, then cutting each half into 5 strips. Thread each strip of chicken onto a skewer, place the skewers in a shallow dish, and pour over the marinade. Cover and set aside in the refrigerator for several hours, preferably overnight.

In a large skillet, heat the oil and pan-sear the chicken skewers for 4 to 6 minutes on each side or until cooked through. Alternatively, arrange the skewers on an oiled baking sheet and place in a preheated 400°F oven for 8 to 10 minutes. Sprinkle a little cracked pepper over the skewered chicken before serving.

2 cloves garlic, finely minced

3 tablespoons ground cumin

1 tablespoon chili powder

1 tablespoon ground coriander

1½ teaspoons paprika

1 cup coconut milk

1½ teaspoons brown sugar

1 teaspoon salt

Three 8-ounce skinless, boneless chicken breasts

Thirty 6- or 8-inch wooden skewers, soaked in water for 1 hour

2 tablespoons vegetable oil

GARNISH
cracked black pepper

GUACAMOLE

T HIS GUACAMOLE IS based on Josefina Howard's famous version from Rosa Mexicano—chunky and with lots of character. It should be made at the last minute for best results, but a little lime juice can be stirred in at the end to keep the avocados from turning brown, enabling you to keep it for several hours. This recipe can be doubled.

4 teaspoons seeded and minced
    fresh jalapeño or serrano pepper
2/3 cup white onion in 1/4-inch dice
3 to 4 tablespoons minced cilantro
3/4 to 1 teaspoon salt
2 medium avocados, preferably
    Haas
6 tablespoons diced tomato, seeds
    and interior ribs removed
1 tablespoon fresh lime juice
    (optional)

Corn chips for serving

In a mortar or stainless steel mixing bowl, combine 2 teaspoons pepper, 1/4 cup onion, 2 teaspoons cilantro, and 1/2 teaspoon salt. Mash with the pestle or the back of a wooden spoon until the mixture forms a wet paste.

To cut the avocado, hold it in one hand and cut a full circle around the seed with a knife, then twist the halves in opposite directions to separate them. With the blade of a heavy knife, strike the top of the seed, give the knife a slight twist, lift the blade, and the seed will come with it. With tip of a small knife, cut the avocado flesh into 1/2-inch dice; do not cut through the skin. Lift the flesh from the skin with a spoon to avoid mashing, and add to the mortar or bowl. Stir gently with the paste.

Add the remaining onion, cilantro, and tomato, and 1 teaspoon peppers at a time, tasting with each addition, and stir carefully. Adjust the seasoning to taste with salt, cilantro, and peppers. Serve immediately with corn chips. Add lime juice if the guacamole is not served immediately.

COLOMBIAN SIRLOIN EMPANADAS WITH AJÍ SAUCE

MAKES 16 TO 18 EMPANADAS

THESE LITTLE STUFFED pastry turnovers containing a savory filling can be found all over South America. Each country has its own variation—some are baked, some fried; some use pastry, others a cornmeal dough. It's very important that you use precooked or instant cornmeal for this recipe, otherwise the dough will not become elastic and easy to roll. The dough, containing almost no fat, will be a little difficult to work with, so be careful when rolling and folding it.

The beef filling for these Colombian sirloin empanadas from Rafael Palomino, chef of Bistro Latino, is quickly sautéed and seasoned at the end with cumin, instead of braised for hours. The empanadas can be made in advance and fried just before serving, but don't leave them around as they will become soggy.

Preheat the oven to 300°F. Place the 2 cloves garlic on a 5-inch square of tinfoil and wrap tightly with the foil. Place on a small baking sheet in the oven and bake for about 30 minutes, until the flesh is very soft. When cool, remove the skins from the garlic.

Blanch the potatoes until al dente; strain and set aside.

While the potatoes are cooking, heat 1 tablespoon olive oil in a sauté pan over medium-high heat. Add the sirloin and cook, stirring, for 5 minutes. Add the scallion, and cook for 1 minute. Add the tomatoes, and cook for 1 minute. Add the potatoes and cumin and stir. Cook for 3 minutes, stirring occasionally. Season to taste with salt and pepper. Cool in refrigerator.

Crush the roasted garlic with 1 teaspoon olive oil and place in a large bowl with the cornmeal, ¼ teaspoon salt, ¼ teaspoon pepper, and the parsley. Pour in the hot stock and stir with a wooden spoon until the ingredients are well combined and the dough is elastic. Add more hot water if mixture is too dry. (Don't overwork the cornmeal, or it won't stick together.) Set the dough in the refrigerator for about 5 minutes—it will become less sticky as it cools.

Cover a large pastry board with a very large sheet of plastic wrap and set the dough on top; cover with another sheet of plastic wrap. Roll the dough out through the wrap to ⅛ inch thick, using short strokes and rolling in one direction only. Using a 3-inch-diameter glass, cut 16 to 18 disks through the wrap. (The wrap shouldn't tear.) Peel the top wrap away

2 cloves unpeeled garlic

1 cup potatoes in ¼-inch dice

1 tablespoon olive oil, plus 1 teaspoon

2 cups sirloin (about 1¼ pounds) in ¼-inch dice

½ cup finely chopped scallion, white part only

1 cup seeded tomatoes in ¼-inch dice

2 teaspoons cumin

Salt and freshly ground black pepper

2 cups superfine cornmeal (precooked), plus a little extra for dusting pastry board

½ tablespoon chopped parsley

1 to 1⅓ cups hot chicken stock or hot water

1 egg, beaten

1 pint vegetable oil for frying

Aji Sauce (recipe follows)

from the disks, and brush disk perimeters with the beaten egg. It is best to remove the dough scraps between the disks at this time, so you'll have more room to work with. Tear off a new sheet of plastic wrap. Move one round at a time to the clean sheet. Place a teaspoon of the beef stuffing on the lower half of each disk; take hold of the plastic wrap and fold it up; the dough will fold with it, to create a half-moon empanada. Use the edge of the glass to press and seal each empanada through the plastic. Remove each empanada from the plastic.

Heat 2 to 3 inches of vegetable oil in a medium-size saucepan over medium-high heat; when hot, drop several empanadas in at a time and cook until pale golden. Remove and drain on a wire rack. Dip them into the Ají Sauce.

AJÍ SAUCE

Avocado is used like butter in many South American countries and is the main ingredient in this wonderful dipping sauce. The ingredients are similar to those in guacamole, but the addition of grated hard-boiled egg gives the sauce a very different appearance.

3 ripe avocados, preferably Haas, peeled, stones removed, and mashed

½ cup coarsely chopped cilantro leaves

1 large tomato, finely diced

3 hard-boiled eggs, coarsely grated

1 teaspoon Tabasco sauce, or to taste

Juice ½ lemon

Salt and freshly ground black pepper

Mix all the ingredients together in a medium-size bowl until well combined and serve with the empanadas.

MERGUEZ KOFTAS WITH TSATSIKI

A LITTLE LARGER THAN meatballs, these hot and spicy Middle Eastern lamb patties are back-yard winners from chef Larry Kolar. Guests can help themselves as the koftas come off the bar-becue, or eat them at room temperature along with the garlic-infused cucumber dipping sauce. Lamb is traditionally used in the Middle East, but beef works well too.

Heat the oil in a skillet over medium heat. Add the onion, garlic, fennel, and pepper flakes. Cook, stirring, until the onion is soft, 3 to 4 minutes, and set aside in a bowl. When cool, add the ground lamb and knead well with your hands. Add parsley, paprika, the spice mix, salt, and pepper and knead to incorporate well. Shape into small patties 1½ to 2 inches in diameter and grill over medium-hot coals. Serve with Tsatsiki and Grilled Za'atar Bread (page 74).

2 teaspoons olive oil
½ onion in ¼-inch dice
½ tablespoon minced garlic
½ fennel bulb in ¼ inch dice
1 tablespoon crushed red pepper flakes
2 pounds ground lamb (30 percent fat)
1 tablespoon chopped parsley
1 tablespoon paprika
2 tablespoons Spice Mix
½ teaspoon salt
¼ teaspoon freshly ground black pepper

SPICE MIX

Toast the fenugreek seed, cinnamon stick, cumin seed, coriander seed, and black peppercorns in a dry skillet over medium heat until they start to give off an aroma, 1 to 2 minutes. Set aside in a bowl, and when cool, grind in a coffee grinder (don't use it again to grind coffee beans as it will flavor the coffee) or with a mortar and pestle.

FOR THE SPICE MIX

1 tablespoon fenugreek seed
   (available in Indian markets)
1 cinnamon stick
¾ teaspoon cumin seed
2 tablespoons coriander seed
1 tablespoon black peppercorns

TSATSIKI

Grate the cucumber and squeeze excess water out of it with your hands. Stir the cucumber and yogurt together in a bowl, add the garlic, and season to taste with salt and pepper.

FOR THE TSATSIKI

1 hothouse or European cucumber,
   unpeeled
16 ounces yogurt, drained overnight
   through paper towel–lined sieve
8 cloves garlic, minced
Salt and freshly ground black pepper

COCKTAILS

THE ERA OF the cocktail has returned. The glass of mediocre white wine is a thing of the past. The following recipes for cocktails, punches, frozen mixes, and even a fruit lemonade will most certainly liven up your next party—whatever the time of the year.

COSMOPOLITAN MARTINI

MAKES 1 SERVING

THE FIFTY SEVEN Fifty Seven Restaurant and Bar in the Four Seasons Hotel is famous for its martinis and creates them for every time of the year, including the Candy Cane Martini for the holiday season.

Shake or stir the ingredients in a cocktail shaker over ice. Strain into a martini glass and garnish with a lime twist.

½ ounce (1 tablespoon) cranberry juice
¼ ounce (1½ teaspoons) Cointreau
4 ounces (½ cup) vodka
Juice of ½ lime

GARNISH
Lime twist

BELLINI MARTINI

MAKES 1 SERVING

Shake or stir the ingredients together over ice in a cocktail shaker. Strain into a martini glass.

3 ounces (6 tablespoons) vodka
½ ounce (1 tablespoon) peach schnapps
½ ounce (1 tablespoon) peach nectar

CANDY CANE MARTINI

MAKES 1 SERVING

Grenadine

Sugar

3 ounces (6 tablespoons) vodka

1 ounce (2 tablespoons) crème de menthe

Small candy cane

Dip the rim of a martini glass in grenadine and then in sugar. Shake or stir together the vodka and crème de menthe with ice in a cocktail shaker. Strain into the prepared martini glass and garnish with a candy cane.

RAINBOW HOLIDAY CUP

MAKES 1 SERVING

MIXOLOGIST DALE DEGROFF from the Rainbow Room came up with the Holiday Cup and the Sparkling Holiday Punch. The spicy holiday cup can be served hot or cold—it's especially good on a wintery evening when served hot. And the Sparkling Holiday Punch solves all the problems when you have children around and need to serve a nonalcoholic drink.

1½ ounces (3 tablespoons) Mount Gay rum

¼ ounce (1½ teaspoons) Goldschläger (cinnamon schnapps)

4 ounces (½ cup) fresh orange juice

2 dashes Angostura bitters

2 dashes grenadine

Splash club soda

GARNISH

1 cinnamon stick

1 orange slice

Pour the ingredients over ice in a stemmed goblet glass. Stir gently. Garnish with a cinnamon stick and orange slice.

SPARKLING HOLIDAY PUNCH

MAKES 1 SERVING

3 ounces (6 tablespoons) orange
  juice
3 ounces (6 tablespoons) pineapple
  juice
½ ounce (1 tablespoon) fresh lemon
  juice
1 ounce (2 tablespoons) strawberry
  syrup
Dash Angostura bitters
3 ounces (6 tablespoons) sparkling
  brut (nonalcoholic)

GARNISH
Sliced orange, lemon, and
  strawberry wheels

Mix together the first five ingredients in a goblet and top with the sparkling brut. Garnish with wheels of orange, lemon, and strawberry.

CHERRY RUM SPECIAL

MAKES 1 SERVING

1 ounce (2 tablespoons) Cherry
  Heering
1 ounce (2 tablespoons) Mount
  Gay rum
2 ounces (4 tablespoons) orange
  juice
2 dashes Angostura bitters

GARNISH
Orange peel

Shake together all of the ingredients with ice in a cocktail shaker and strain into a frozen martini glass. Garnish with an orange peel.

COOL JAVA

JERRY'S, THE SOHO restaurant, finds that Cool Java makes an ideal after-dinner drink, combining brandy, Triple Sec, and black coffee topped with a dollop of whipped cream.

Mix together the ingredients with ice in a cocktail shaker, then strain into a cocktail glass. Top with whipped cream and a sprinkle of cocoa powder if desired.

1 ounce (2 tablespoons) brandy
1 ounce (2 tablespoons) Triple Sec
1 ounce (2 tablespoons) cold black
    coffee

GARNISH
Whipped cream, cocoa powder

FROZEN MINT CAIPIRINHA

MAKES 2 SERVINGS

FROZEN DRINKS ARE great summer coolers and make the most of fresh fruit and herbs. A strong blender is a must for these drinks, and if you are thinking of serving them for a large crowd, it is a good idea to have an ice cream maker on hand where you can keep the blended frozen drinks until the guests arrive. The Mint Caipirinha created by the Candy Bar and Grill is based on *cachaca,* a Brazilian spirit distilled from sugar cane.

Place the ice in a blender, followed by the remaining ingredients. Blend at low speed for 5 seconds, then on high until the mixture is firm. (Add a little more ice if the mixture is not firm enough.)

Pour into martini glasses and garnish with sprigs of mint.

1 cup ice
2 ounces (4 tablespoons) *cachaca*
¼ cup Simple Syrup (page 120)
2 ounces (4 tablespoons) fresh
    lime juice
10 mint leaves

GARNISH
Mint sprigs

RUM PUNCH

ONE OF SOUR, two of sweet, three of strong, and four of weak—this is my husband's favorite version of a traditional West Indian Rum Punch. It tastes harmless but has quite a kick!

In a cocktail shaker, combine the lime juice and sugar, stirring until the sugar has dissolved. Add the rum and water and pour into a tumbler filled with ice. A "floater" of Goslings Black Seal Rum can be added if desired. Grate a little fresh nutmeg over the top of the punch.

Juice of 1 lime
2 teaspoons instant dissolving sugar
  or Simple Syrup (page 120)
3 ounces (6 tablespoons) rum
4 ounces (½ cup) water
Goslings Black Seal Rum (optional)

GARNISH
Whole nutmeg

RITZ FIZZ

THE COLOR ALONE of this drink is appealing, even more so when the fizz is served in an old-fashioned saucer-shaped champagne glass.

Chill a champagne flute or preferably a "Marie Antoinette" saucer-type champagne glass. Mix the Curaçao, Amaretto, and the lemon juice together and top with champagne. Garnish with the orange twist.

¼ ounce (1½ teaspoons) blue
  Curaçao
¼ ounce (1½ teaspoons) Amaretto
Juice of ¼ lemon
Champagne or sparkling wine

GARNISH
Orange twist

PISCO SOUR

FELL IN love with this drink on a recent trip to Chile and it is great to serve on a summer's day. Pisco, a fermented grape juice, is becoming more readily available, but if your local liquor store doesn't stock it, demand it! The egg white gives the drink a wonderful frothy finish and allows the Angostura bitters to float on top.

2 cups pisco (35 percent)
¼ cup Simple Syrup (page 120)
½ cup fresh lemon juice
½ teaspoon lemon zest, finely
    grated
1 egg white
Angostura bitters

Combine the first five ingredients with ice in the blender and blend for a few minutes until the ice is crushed. Pour into flutes and add a dash of Angostura bitters to the top of each drink. Serve immediately.

PIMM'S CUP

THIS IS A great English favorite in the summer—especially during the Wimbledon championships and Henley Regatta. It is usually combined with a fizzy lemon soda—the closest you can find in America is Sprite, which is a little sweeter. Ginger ale can also be used.

4 ounces Pimm's
12 ounces lemon soda, such as
    Sprite, 7-Up, or ginger ale
Ice

GARNISH
Slices of orange, strips of unwaxed
    cucumber peel, a sprig of
    flowering borage or a sprig
    of fresh mint

Pour the Pimm's and the soda into a tumbler, add ice cubes, and garnish with slices of orange and cucumber and borage or mint. For a party, the quantities can be quadrupled and drinks served from a large pitcher.

FROZEN PEACH BELLINI

MAKES 2 SERVINGS

FRESH SUMMER PEACHES with the addition of peach sorbet intensify the texture and flavor of chef Mark Strausman's frozen Bellini.

2 fresh peaches, peeled and pitted

1 scoop peach sorbet

1 cup ice

1 cup cold Prosecco or other
    sparkling wine

Place all the ingredients in a blender and blend at high speed until the ice is crushed. Turn off the blender, and allow the Bellini to rest for 20 seconds. Pour into champagne glasses.

FROZEN TEQUILA LIMEADE

MAKES 1 SERVING

THE ADDITION OF chopped lime zest makes Bobby Flay's frozen tequila limeade extra tart, and a refreshing twist on the traditional margarita.

2 ounces (¼ cup) silver tequila

Juice of 1 lime

2 tablespoons Simple Syrup
    (page 120) or to taste

1 teaspoon finely chopped lime zest

¾ cup ice

GARNISH

Lime slice

Place all the ingredients in a blender and blend until smooth. Pour into a large wineglass, garnish with the lime slice, and serve immediately.

BUCKS FIZZ

A POPULAR ENGLISH EYE-OPENER similar to a mimosa, but the addition of Cointreau gives it a little more of a kick! You don't need to use good champagne for the fizz, as long as it's dry.

Mix the orange juice with the champagne in a large jug, and finish with the Cointreau. Garnish each glass with a slice of orange.

1½ cups orange juice, freshly
    squeezed
1 bottle champagne or dry
    sparkling wine
¼ cup Cointreau

GARNISH
Orange slices

VIN D'ORANGE

V IN D'ORANGE COMBINES my favorite summer wine, *rosé de Provence,* with oranges. Serve it as an aperitif over ice and dream of fields of lavender.

Strip off the orange rind with a vegetable peeler and add to the wine. Recork the bottle and set aside in a cool place for 15 days. Strain the wine, stir in the cognac and sugar, and serve.

4 medium oranges
1 bottle rosé wine (preferably
    Provençal)
½ cup cognac
½ cup sugar

RASPBERRY LEMONADE

NOT QUITE THE lemonade you grew up with, but this creation from the Four Seasons Hotel in Manhattan is an amazingly refreshing drink for those dog days of summer. Other fruits such as strawberries or blueberries can be substituted, but the sugar will have to be adjusted.

2 pints raspberries
1 cup sugar
2 cups fresh lemon juice
4 cups water

GARNISH
Sprig of mint, raspberries

Puree the fruit with the sugar in a blender. Strain the puree into a pitcher. Add the lemon juice and water. Stir well and pour into ice-filled glasses. Garnish with a sprig of mint and a raspberry.

SIMPLE SYRUP

INSTEAD OF USING sugar, which is difficult to dissolve, a simple syrup sweetens a drink much more effectively. It will keep indefinitely in the refrigerator.

3 cups water
6 cups sugar

Heat the water and sugar in a saucepan over medium heat until the sugar dissolves. Increase the heat and boil for 1 to 2 minutes. Refrigerate when cool.

MAIL-ORDER SOURCES

Adriana's Caravan
409 Vanderbilt Street
Brooklyn, NY 11218
1-800-316-0820
Herbs and spices and chiles

Balducci's
424 Avenue of the Americas
New York, NY 10011
Tel: 800-BALDUCCI
Fax: 516-843-0383
Gourmet food products

Coyote Café, General Store
132 West Water Street
Santa Fe, NM 87501
Tel: 505-982-2454
800-866-HOWL (4695)
Southwestern food products

Dean and DeLuca
560 Broadway
New York, NY 10012-3938
212-226-6800
1-800-221-7714
http://www.dean-deluca.com
Gourmet food products

Foods of India
121 Lexington Avenue
New York, NY 10016
Tel: 212-683-4419
Fax: 212-251-0946
Indian food products

Kalustyan's
123 Lexington Avenue
New York, NY 10016
212-685-3451
Herbs and spices, nuts, preserved
lemons, and Middle Eastern foods

Katagiri
224 East 59th Street
New York, NY 10022
Tel: 212-755-3566
Fax: 212-752-4197
Japanese food products

Kitchen/Market
218 Eighth Avenue
New York, NY 10011
Tel: 212-243-4433
888-468-4433
Southwestern food products

Mo Hotta-Mo Betta
P.O. Box 4136
San Luis Obispo, CA 93403
800-462-3220
Fax 800-618-4454
Hot and spicy food products

Murray's Cheese Shop
257 Bleecker Street
New York, NY 10014
888-692-4339
Wonderful cheeses

Myers of Keswick
634 Hudson Street
New York, NY 10014
Tel: 212-691-4194
Fax: 212-691-7423
English products including homemade
Cumberland sausage meat

Penzeys, Ltd.
P.O. Box 933
Muskego, WI 53150
Tel: 414-574-0277
Fax: 414-574-0278
Herbs and spices

Shallah's Middle East Importing Company
290 White Street
Danbury, CT 06810
203-743-4181
Middle Eastern food products

Uwajimaya (Mainly Japanese)
519 Sixth Avenue South
Seattle, WA 98104
Tel: 206-624-6248
Fax: 206-624-6915
Mainly Japanese food products

INDEX